D0531949

Knitted and Felted Toys

Knitted and Felted Toys

26 easy-to-knit patterns for adorable toys

ZOË HALSTEAD

kp krause publications
An Imprint of F+W Publications, Inc.
www.krausebooks.com

This book is dedicated to my two best boys: Elliot and Leo

First published in North America
by Krause Publications
an imprint of F+W Publications, Inc.
700 East State Street
Iola, Wisconsin 54990-0001
(888) 457-2873

First Published in Great Britain in 2007 by
New Holland Publishers (UK) Ltd

ISBN-13: 978-0-89689-587-4
ISBN-10: 0-89689-587-4

Reproduction by Pica Digital PTE Ltd, Singapore
Printed and bound by Times Offset, Malaysia

Contents

Introduction

I was taught to knit by my Gran when I was five and I can still vividly remember the short red plastic needles and blue wool. My first project was a scarf for my teddy, and there then followed various blankets, jumpers, clothes, and toys as I fell in love with the endless possibilities of knitting.

It was only natural that a degree in textiles, and a career designing within the knitwear and spinning industry should follow. Having designed for, and tried my hand at various other needlecrafts since, hand knitting will always remain my first love!

This book is a collection of over 25 adorable knitted toys. Hand knitted fabric lends itself so perfectly to toys; it's inherent softness and pliability is just waiting to be touched and cuddled. What could be nicer to welcome a new arrival, than a handmade toy, or to indulge an adored child, grandchild or friend, than a lovable knitted companion?

There is something for everyone here, from Leo Lion with his bright spots and loopy mane; the Ballerina with her pretty tutu and ballet shoes; Ellie Flowers with her felted flower pattern; and the soft garter stitch Poppy Pig. There is a skill level indicator for each design with easy patterns to tempt beginners, and plenty to appeal to the more experienced knitter.

Half the toys in the book have been made from yarn that has been felted after it has been knitted. Felting produces a wonderfully soft and fluffy fabric to add a new dimension to your toy knitting. There are full instructions on how to felt on pages 16–17, so if you haven't tried this exciting technique before, now's your chance.

Each toy has been beautifully photographed and each set of instructions includes all the information you will need to complete the toy; from material requirements, through full knitting instructions, to complete making up and finishing information.

In designing the toys I have really enjoyed using different yarn textures and colors, as I wanted the toys to be fun to make, with quirky and cute results. I hope you enjoy knitting and creating these toys as much as I have enjoyed dreaming them up!

Getting started

The pages that follow contain all the information you need to help you create beautiful knitted and felted toys, from yarns and equipment to basic techniques.

KNITTED FABRICS

All knitted fabrics are made using just two basic stitches, knit and purl.

GARTER STITCH (g st)

This is when every row is knitted in the same stitch, either knit every row, or purl every row. This produces a reversible fabric with horizontal ridges that does not curl at the edges.

STOCKINETTE STITCH (st st)

This is the most widely used knitted fabric. Alternate rows are knitted, the others are purled. With the knit side as the right side, the fabric is smooth and flat. With the purl side as the right side (referred to as reverse stockinette stitch) the fabric has horizontal ridges which are closer together than in garter stitch. Stockinette stitch will curl at the edges and, therefore, needs borders or seams to keep it flat.

SEED STITCH

This is a textured stitch made up of alternate knit and purl stitches. Stitches that are knitted on one row will be knitted again on the next row. Stitches that are purled on one row will, again, be purled on the next. This produces a reversible, textured fabric that does not curl at the edges.

GAUGE

For each pattern there is a recommended gauge. It can seem like a chore to have to knit a gauge square, but it is extremely important as it can make the difference between a great looking toy that is perfect in size and shape, and one that is disappointing. The gauge for the plain knitted toys needs to be fairly tight to result in a firm fabric that can be stuffed well. Too loose a gauge will result in an open fabric through which stuffing will show. Too tight a gauge will result in a stiff looking toy without much pliability.

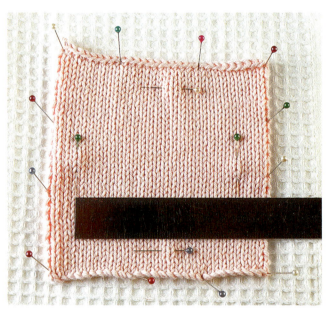

Above: *checking gauge*

Above: *garter stitch*

Above: *stockinette stitch*

Above: *seed stitch*

Before starting a project, knit a gauge square 5–10 more stitches and 5–10 more rows than stated in the gauge note. Lay the finished square on a flat surface and smooth out, taking care not to distort the stitches. Use a ruler or metal tape measure to measure a 4 in. (10 cm) square. Using pins as markers, pin vertically between stitches and horizontally between rows. Count the number of stitches and rows between the markers. If you have more stitches and rows than is stated in the gauge note, you are knitting too tightly and you will need to try again with needles that are one size larger. If you have too few stitches and rows you are knitting too loosely and you will need to try again with needles that are one size smaller. Once you have achieved the correct gauge your toy will be knitted to the measurements given at the beginning of each pattern.

NEEDLES

Knitting needles are available in a variety of materials from aluminium to wood, and come in sizes ranging from 2 mm to 10 mm and beyond. They also come in a variety of lengths – what you use depends on personal preference. However, you may find it easier to use shorter needles for toy projects.

While knitting and making up projects, you will also find the following equipment useful: a tape measure, safety pins, bobbins for color knitting, scissors, pins, and tapestry needles for sewing seams.

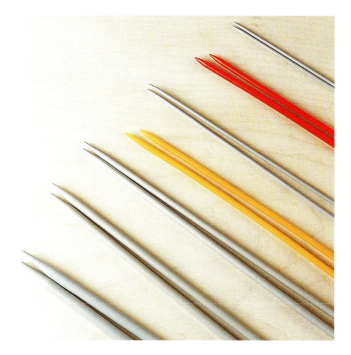

Above: *knitting needles come in a range of sizes*

Left: *you will also need a tape measure, pins, small scissors, tapestry needles, safety pins, and yarn bobbins*

KNITTING NEEDLE CONVERSION TABLE

US	Metric	UK/Canada
0	2 mm	14
1	2¼ mm	13
2	2¾ mm	12
2/3	3 mm	11
3	3¼ mm	10
5	3¾ mm	9
6	4 mm	8
7	4½ mm	7
8	5 mm	6
9	5½ mm	5
10	6 mm	4
10½	6½ mm	3
10½	7 mm	2
11	7½ mm	1
11	8 mm	0
13	9 mm	00
15	10 mm	000

GLOSSARY OF UK AND US TERMINOLOGY

The following are the few differences between UK and US knitting terms:

US	UK/Canada
bind off	cast off
shade	color
gauge	tension
seed stitch	moss stitch
stockinette stitch	stocking stitch
finish	make up
yarn over (yo)	yarn over needle
yarn over (yo)	yarn forward
yarn over (yo)	yarn round needle

ABBREVIATIONS

The following are the general abbreviations used in the patterns:

alt	alternate
beg	begin(ning)
ch	chain stitch (crochet)
cm	centimeters
cont	continu(e)(ing)
dc	double crochet
dec	decreas(e)(ing)
foll	following
g st	garter stitch (k every row)
in.	inch(es)
inc	increase(e)(ing)
k	knit
m1	make one, by picking up the bar between last stitch and the next and working into the back of it
meas	measures
mm	millimeter(s)
p	purl
patt	pattern
psso	pass slipped stitch over
rem	remain(ing)
rep	repeat(s)(ing)
rev st st	reverse stockinette stitch
RS	right side
skpo	slip 1, knit 1, pass slipped stitch over
sl 1	slip one stitch
ss	slip stich (crochet)
st(s)	stitch(es)
st st	stockinette stitch (RS row k, WS row p)
tbl	through back of loop(s)
tog	together
tr	treble
WS	wrong side
yb	yarn back
yfwd	yarn forward
yon	yarn over needle
yrn	yarn round needle
*	repeat instructions between asterisks as many times as instructed
[]	work instructions inside [ ]s as many times as instructed

Above: *knitting yarns are now available in a wide range of colors and textures*

YARNS

Throughout this book, where possible, double knitting yarns have been used so that color changes can be very easily made. With the dolls in particular, always bear in mind the child for which the toy is intended, and alter the skin tone, hair color and clothes accordingly. Any child will delight in a truly individual toy made specifically for them.

Please do experiment with different colorways and combinations to ring the changes in any of the other toys too. However, each yarn has been chosen as the best for that particular toy. Therefore, if you do substitute different yarn types, please be sure to knit a gauge square to make sure you are happy with the different effect it may produce. Also, it is always best to substitute yarns with a similar yardage/meterage, so that the resulting toy is as close as possible to the original design. Please note: some of the toys have 100 g balls listed in the requirements, this is because the yarn is only available in that weight of ball but the toy will not use all of the yarn. Therefore, if you do use a substitute yarn, you may only need a fraction of 100 g.

YARN WEIGHT CONVERSION TABLE

UK/Canada	US
4 ply	Sport
Double knitting	Light worsted
Aran	Fisherman/Worsted
Chunky	Bulky
Super Chunky	Extra Bulky

YARN INFORMATION
YARNS FOR PLAIN KNITTING

Jaeger Matchmaker Merino DK: a 100% Merino Wool double knitting yarn. Approximately 131 yd (120 m) per 50 g (1¾ oz) ball.

King Cole Big Value DK: a 100% Premium Acrylic double knitting yarn. Approximately 320 yd (290 m) per 100 g (3½ oz) ball.

King Cole Big Value Baby DK: a 100% Premium Acrylic double knitting yarn. Approximately 316 yd (289 m) per 100 g (3½ oz) ball.

King Cole Petal DK: a double knitting yarn (85% minimum Premium acrylic). Approximately 296 yd (260 m) per 100 g (3½ oz) ball.

King Cole Woolmix DK: a double knitting yarn (75% Premium Acrylic, 25% Wool). Approximately 295 yd (270 m) per 100 g (3½ oz) ball.

King Cole Sprinkles: a medium weight, fancy yarn (100% Polyester). Approximately 65 yd (60 m) per 50 g (1¾ oz) ball.

Peter Pan Darling: a medium weight velvet effect yarn (100% Polyester). Approximately 122 yd (112 m) per 50 g (1¾ oz) ball.

Rowan Calmer: a lofty, soft, medium weight yarn (75% Cotton, 25% Acrylic/microfiber). Approximately 175 yd (160 m) per 50 g (1¾ oz) ball.

Rowan Spray: a soft, chunky yarn (60% Wool, 40% Acrylic). Approximately 87 yd (80 m) per 100 g (3½ oz) ball.

Sirdar Country Style DK: a double knitting yarn (45% Acrylic, 40% Nylon, 15% Wool). Approximately 347 yd (318 m) per 100 g (3½ oz) ball.

Sirdar Snuggly Pearls DK: a double knitting yarn (53% Nylon, 43% Acrylic, 4% Polyester). Approximately 185 yd (170 m) per 50 g (1¾ oz) ball.

Sirdar Luxury Soft Cotton DK: a 100% Cotton double knitting yarn. Approximately 103 yd (95 m) per 50 g (1¾ oz) ball.

Sirdar Medici: a fancy effect yarn (70% Nylon, 28% Cotton, 2% Polyester). Approximately 103 yd (95 m) per 50 g (1¾ oz) ball.

Sirdar Bonus Toytime DK: a 100% Acrylic double knitting yarn. Approximately 76 yd (70 m) per 25 g (1 oz) ball.

Twilleys of Stamford Freedom Cotton DK: a 100% Cotton double knitting yarn. Approximately 93 yd (85 m) per 50 g (1¾ oz) ball.

Twilleys of Stamford Lyscordet: a 100% Mercerised Cotton yarn, equivalent to 3 ply. Approximately 437 yd (400 m) per 100 g (3½ oz) ball.

Twilleys of Stamford Goldfingering: a metallic yarn, equivalent to 3 ply (80% Viscose, 20% Metallised Polyester. Approximately 109 yd (100 m) per 25 g (1 oz) ball.
Wendy Courtelle DK: a 100% Courtelle Acrylic double knitting yarn. Approximately 82 yd (75 m) per 25 g (1 oz) ball.

YARNS FOR FELTED KNITTING

Alpaca Select DK: a 100% Alpaca double knitting yarn. Approximately 109 yd (100 m) per 50 g (1¾ oz) ball.
Rowan Scottish Tweed 4 ply: a 100% Pure New Wool 4-ply yarn. Approximately 120 yd (110 m) per 25 g (1 oz) ball.
Rowan Scottish Tweed Chunky: a 100% Pure New Wool chunky yarn. Approximately 109 yd (100 m) per 100 g (3½ oz) ball.
Shetland Wool Brokers 2 ply Jumper Weight: a 100% Pure Shetland Wool yarn equivalent to 4 ply. Approximately 129 yd (118 m) per 25 g (1 oz) ball.
UK Alpaca DK Yarn: a double knit yarn (70% Fine UK Alpaca, 30% British Blueface Leicester Wool). Approximately 289 yd (265 m) per 100 g (3½ oz) ball.

BASIC SHAPING

All of the projects in this book contain basic shaping techniques. Shaping is achieved by increasing and decreasing during knitting to form the fabric into the required shape. The methods I have used are described below.

INCREASING

Increasing the number of stitches in a row is achieved by either of the following:
Make one (m1): pick up the horizontal bar in between this stitch and the next with your right needle. Place it onto your left needle and then knit into the back loop.
Increase knit wise (inc): knit into the front loop of the stitch as normal but do not slip the stitch off the left needle. Instead knit into the back loop of the same stitch.

DECREASING

Decreasing the number of stitches in a row is achieved by either of the following:
Skpo: slip one stitch (pass a stitch without knitting it onto your right needle), knit the next stitch then, using the point of the left needle, lift the slipped stitch over the knitted stitch.
K2tog: place the point of the right needle into the front loops of the first two stitches on the left needle and knit both loops at the same time.

Above: *increasing by making one (m1)*

Above: *increasing knitwise into front and back of same stitch (inc)*

Above: *decreasing by skpo*

Above: *decreasing by knitting 2 stitches together (k2tog)*

COLOR KNITTING

There are two main methods of working different colors in knitted fabric: intarsia and fairisle. The intarsia technique is usually used where a block of color is required in just one area of the row, and there is usually a chart to follow for this. The fairisle technique is used when a pattern is repeated across the row, working different colors a few stitches at a time.

INTARSIA

For the intarsia technique it is best to have small lengths, balls or bobbins of yarn for each area of color along the row. This produces a single thickness of fabric and the yarn is not carried across the back of the knitting so that the motif does not become distorted. Join in the various colors at the appropriate point in the row, and to avoid gaps in the knitting as you change color, twist the yarns around each other on the wrong side. All ends can then be darned in at the end or knitted in as you work.

FAIRISLE

With the fairisle technique, the yarns are carried across the back and used every few stitches to form a repeating pattern (this technique is used for the Cowboy's checked shirt, see page 121). If the yarn has to carry over more than 3 stitches it's best to catch it in at the back, with the yarn you're knitting with at the time, to avoid long loops on the reverse. Try not to pull the yarns too tightly, as this will distort the fabric.

CHARTS

Some of the patterns in the book contain charts for intarsia knitting. Each square on the chart represents one stitch and each line of squares represents one row of knitting. When working from the charts, read odd rows (K) from right to left, and even rows (P) from left to right. Each color used is given a different symbol and these are shown in the key alongside each chart.

Above: *intarsia – English method*

Above: *intarsia – continental method*

Above: *fairisle – English method*

Above: *fairisle – continental method*

MAKING UP AND FINISHING

Please spend time finishing and making up well, as although the process can be time consuming, the resulting toy will be a professional looking one.

PRESSING

When you have finished knitting all the pieces of your toy, sew in all the yarn ends neatly.

Most of the shaped pieces, and those using acrylic yarns, are best not pressed. Any lumps and bumps should be smoothed away when the toy is stuffed. However, any garments would benefit from being blocked and pressed lightly beneath a dry cloth to aid making up. Please refer to ball band instructions if you are at all unsure about pressing.

BACKSTITCH

Unless otherwise stated, backstitch is good for sewing up the majority of the toys in this book. With stripes and patterns, make sure to match the edges well.

Place the two pieces of knitting right sides together and pin in place. Thread a length of the correct colored yarn into a large-eyed, darning needle and secure it to the knitting where you want to begin stitching. Bring the needle up through both pieces of knitting, to the front one row up from the bottom of the knitting. Take the needle back down to the bottom edge and insert it, then bring it back up two rows up from the bottom edge. Insert back in at the top of the first stitch and then back out two rows up. Continue in this way so that every stitch is one row down and two rows up, until the end of the seam. Fasten off.

Use the ridges and lines of the knitting to guide you so that your seams are kept straight.

MATTRESS STITCH

Use mattress stitch to join center back body and leg seams and any other seam where you want a particularly neat finish, as it produces a virtually invisible seam.

Thread a length of the correct colored yarn into a large eyed, darning needle and secure it to one piece of knitting where you want to begin stitching. Bring the needle to the front between the first and second stitches. Now lay both pieces of knitting to be joined with right sides facing you. Insert the needle between the first two stitches on the other piece and then again on the first piece. Keep stitching in this way, forming a neat zig zag of stitches between the two pieces and pulling the knitted pieces together every few stitches, until you reach the end of the seam. Fasten off.

STUFFING

Always use washable toy stuffing that conforms to all safety regulations to stuff your toys. The golden rule with stuffing is; moderation. Overstuffing will distort the fabric and make the toy stiff, board-like and heavy. Understuffing will result in a limp, sad looking toy.

SAFETY

Please bear in mind the age of the recipient of each toy that you make. For young children and babies; make sure that no buttons, plastic eyes or extra items are used that could become loose and be swallowed. Embroider all features and sew everything as securely as possible.

Above: *back stitch*

Above: *mattress stitch*

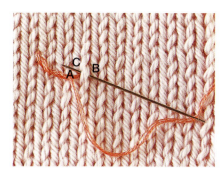

Above: *stem stitch*

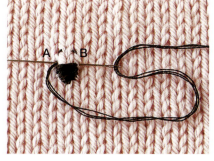

Above: *satin stitch*

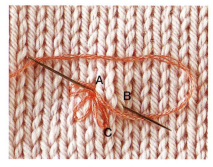

Above: *lazy daisy stitch*

EMBROIDERY STITCHES

Throughout the book, stranded embroidery thread has been used to provide fine detail and definition to the features of all the toys. The following are the main embroidery stitches used.

STEM STITCH

This is mainly used for mouths and noses.

Bring needle out at A, insert back at B and emerge at C (halfway between A and B). Continue in this way, making short, slightly angled, and overlapping stitches, working from left to right.

SATIN STITCH

Satin stitch is mainly used for eyes, noses and nostrils.

Bring the needle out at A and insert at B. Continue in this way working across the area to be covered either straight across or at an angle, making sure not to pull the stitches too tight and keeping neat edges to the stitched area. It sometimes helps to work a line of chain stitches or running stitches around the area to be filled with satin stitch, so that the edges remain neat.

LAZY DAISY STITCH

This decorative stitch is used on the Upside Down Dolly's skirt (see page 82). Bring the needle out at A. Insert back at A, and emerge at B, looping the yarn under the tip of the needle. Pull needle through and over loop and insert at C. Emerge at A for next stitch.

ADDITIONAL TECHNIQUES

Some of the toys have scarves and hats that require fringing and pom poms.

FRINGING

Cut the yarn to the required lengths. With the wrong side of the knitted fabric facing you, insert a crochet hook from the front to the back. Fold the yarn in half, place the loop on the

hook and pull the loop of yarn through. Thread the ends of yarn through the loop and pull to make a knot against the edge of the knitted fabric. Continue as per the instructions given for that particular toy's scarf.

POM-POMS

To make pom-poms it is easiest to use one of the kits that are readily available. The kits usually contain plastic semi-circles that clip together and allow you to wind your chosen yarn around. You then cut the yarn and remove the plastic parts to use again. Alternatively, you can use cardboard circles and make pom-poms in the conventional way.

Above: *fringing*

Above: *pom-pom kits*

Felting information

As you will notice, half the toys in this book have been made from knitting that has been felted. Traditionally, the term "felting" is only applied to raw, carded wool which is washed with soap and water to form a fluffy, matted fabric. When the same process is applied to knitted fabric it is called "fulling". The combination of hot and cold water, soap, and agitation causes the fibers in the yarn to fluff, burst and matt slightly. Fulled fabric, therefore, is more dense, soft and warm to wear as it is less penetrable than ordinary knitted fabric. For the purposes of this book, however, I shall continue to refer to the process as felting.

YARNS

Most 100% wool, alpaca, mohair, or animal fiber blends will felt well. However, it is best to avoid any 100% wool yarns that are labelled "machine washable" or "superwash" as these have been chemically treated so that the fibers will not burst or matt, however roughly they are treated. Also, certain colors, in particular heather mixtures, felt much less quickly than others.

GAUGE

For all of the felted toys in this book you will notice that the gauge is deliberately loose. This is to allow for the shrinkage that will occur when the knitting is felted. Most knitted pieces will shrink much more in length than in width and this has been accounted for.

I cannot stress enough the importance of gauge swatch knitting, especially as the knitting is going to be felted.

Above: *examples of yarns for felting*

I know it can seem like a chore to have to knit and then felt a gauge swatch, when you've got your heart set on knitting that cute, felted chap, but it can save you from some very costly mistakes. I know the disastrous results that can be had from not testing gauge swatches in my washing machine.

When you knit a gauge square for felting, it is a good idea to mark the 4 in. (10 cm) square area with markers made from a yarn that will not felt (e.g. cotton). In this way, after washing, you will clearly be able to see how much shrinkage has occurred over the area without having to try and count stitches and rows that have become blurred by felting.

Try experimenting with any oddments of 100% wool, or wool blend, yarns that you have and see what results you get. Make sure to make notes on everything you do so that you can work out the shrinkage and repeat the process for a toy.

METHOD

There are two main ways of felting knitted fabric; either by hand or in the washing machine.

Felting by hand allows you to control the level to which your knitting is felted and therefore, allows you to stop when you reach the desired level.

Felting by machine, while producing good results in the main, is more variable as different makes of washing

Above: *gauge swatches showing before felting (left) and after felting (right). Note the pink yarn markers*

machine vary so greatly. Also, you only see the results at the end of the wash cycle by which time it may be too late! If you have a top loading washing machine, you may find machine felting much easier. You are able to periodically stop the wash cycle and fish out your knitted pieces to check on their progress, continuing until you are happy with the results.

Most of the toys in this book have been felted by hand, but the following instructions include both methods.

HOW TO FELT KNITTING IN THE WASHING MACHINE

You will need:

- Knitted pieces with all the ends sewn in
- Soap rather than detergent, it can be liquid or flakes but look for 'soap' on the label
- Jeans or an item of clothing that will withstand being washed at 140°F (60°C) (not towels as the lint transfers)
- Washing machine
- Towel for drying

1 Place the knitted pieces in the washing machine with the jeans (this aids the agitation), and the soap, and wash on a 140°F (60°C) wash cycle.
2 When the cycle has finished, remove the knitted pieces and gently tease the matted edges apart, and reshape.
3 Squeeze out any excess water by rolling the pieces in a towel.
4 Dry supported on a towel, out of direct sunlight.

HOW TO FELT KNITTING BY HAND

You will need:

- Knitted pieces with all the ends sewn in
- Soap rather than detergent, it can be liquid or flakes, but look for 'soap' on the label
- Two large shallow bowls (or sink and a large bowl)
- Pair of thick rubber gloves
- Hot and cold water
- Ice cubes
- Towel for drying

1 Fill the sink, or one bowl, with just boiled water and, wearing the rubber gloves, carefully add a handful of soap flakes or liquid and stir. Place the knitted pieces in the water and, making sure they're completely covered, leave to soak for a few minutes.
2 Meanwhile, fill the other bowl with cold water and ice cubes.
3 Begin to knead, rub and agitate the knitted pieces vigorously in the hot water, taking care not to scald yourself.
4 Then switch to the cold water bowl and continue rubbing and agitating. Felting may happen quickly, or it may take several switches between the hot and the cold water.
5 Make sure to rub the piece evenly all over to retain the shape. Cords can be rolled between the hands to encourage felting.
6 Keep the temperature of each bowl of water to its optimum level so that the knitting felts quickly.
7 When you have achieved your desired level of felting, rinse the pieces well. Squeeze out any excess water by rolling the pieces in a towel.
8 Dry supported on a towel, out of direct sunlight.

TIMINGS

Each pattern states how long, and which method of felting, is required. The figure represents the total time spent on the process, felting all the pieces for that toy together.

I prefer a lightly felted appearance to retain a little stitch definition. However, if you prefer a more felted look, then continue with the process until you reach the desired level. Please be aware that the more you felt the pieces the thicker they will become and the smaller the resulting toy will be.

Left: *equipment required for hand felting*

Mice Twice

Or even thrice! These mice are an ideal way of using up oddments of wool for a first felting project. Why not knit a few to decorate the desk of a loved one?

felted knitting

★
☆
☆

SKILL LEVEL:
easy

MEASUREMENTS
Approximately 4¾ in. (12 cm) long (body only)

MATERIALS
- Oddments of UK Alpaca in Rose, Turquoise and Moss
- Pair of US 7 (4½ mm) knitting needles
- Stranded embroidery thread in Black and White
- Washable toy stuffing

ABBREVIATIONS
See page 10.

GAUGE
20 sts and 26 rows to 4 in. (10 cm) measured over stockinette stitch using US 7 (4½ mm) needles, before hand felting.

MOUSE

BODY
With US 7 (4½ mm) needles and color of your choice, cast on 12 sts.
Beg with a k row, work 2 rows in st st.
Next row: [K1, m1] to last st, k1. (23 sts.)
P 1 row.
Next row: K8, [m1, k2] 4 times, k7. (27 sts.)
P 1 row.
Next row: K9, [m1, k1] 10 times, k8. (37 sts.)
Beg with a p row, work 17 rows in st st.
Next row: K8, [k1, k2tog] 7 times, k8. (30 sts.)
P 1 row.
Next row: K8, [k2tog] 7 times, k8. (23 sts.)
P 1 row.

Beg with a k row, work 10 rows in st st, dec 1 st at each end of every row. (3 sts.)
Break yarn, thread through rem sts, draw up tightly and fasten off.

EARS (Make 2)
With US 7 (4½ mm) needles and color of your choice, cast on 6 sts.
Beg with a k row, work 4 rows in st st.
Bind off.

FELTING INSTRUCTIONS
Work in all ends with a needle.
Following the instructions on page 17 for hand felting, felt all pieces for approximately 25 minutes.
Note: This yarn will not withstand machine felting.
Reshape while damp, and dry thoroughly.

TO MAKE UP

Note: Purl side is right side.

Sew seam along length of body, leaving the cast-on edge open for stuffing. Stuff firmly and close opening.

Sew ears to top of head in line with decreases.

Embroider eyes and nose in satin stitch, using black embroidery thread. Sew a small white highlight in each eye.

Tail

Cut 6 x 12 in. (30 cm) lengths of yarn and loop through the bottom of the mouse with a crochet hook. Pull the lengths through until there are equal lengths on each side. Divide the lengths into 3 groups of 4 lengths each and plait to the end. Knot and trim.

Right: *the mice have plaited tails*

Below: *three sweet mice*

Shape String

Designed to be strung across a buggy, pram or cot; this shape string would be a lovely gift for a new arrival. Why not put a bell in one of the shapes to gently tinkle as baby bats it?

felted knitting

★
☆
☆

SKILL LEVEL:
easy

MEASUREMENTS
Approximately 20 in. (50 cm) long

MATERIALS
- 1 x 25 g ball of Shetland Wool Brokers 2 ply Jumper Weight in Cream 1A
- 1 x 25 g ball of Shetland Wool Brokers 2 ply Jumper Weight in Yellow 96
- 1 x 25 g ball of Shetland Wool Brokers 2 ply Jumper Weight in Pink 101
- 1 x 25 g ball of Shetland Wool Brokers 2 ply Jumper Weight in Pale Blue 14
- 1 x 25 g ball of Shetland Wool Brokers 2 ply Jumper Weight in Lilac 49
- 1 x 25 g ball of Shetland Wool Brokers 2 ply Jumper Weight in Turquoise 75
- Pair of US 9 (5½ mm) knitting needles
- Washable toy stuffing

ABBREVIATIONS
See page 10.

GAUGE
16 sts and 23 rows to 4 in. (10 cm) measured over stockinette stitch using US 9 (5½ mm) needles and 2 strands of yarn, before hand felting.

Note: Two strands of yarn are used together, throughout, for all pieces.

THE SHAPES

CUBES
Face (Make 2 Pink, 2 Blue)

With 5½ mm (UK 5/US 9) needles and 2 strands of chosen color, cast on 10 sts.
Beg with a k row, work 16 rows in st st.
Bind off.

Sides (Make 1 Pink, 1 Blue)

With 5½ mm (UK 5/US 9) needles and 2 strands of chosen color, cast on 10 sts.
Beg with a k row, work 56 rows in st st.
Bind off.

TRIANGLE
Face (Make 2)

With 5½ mm (UK 5/US 9) needles and 2 strands of Yellow, cast on 12 sts.
Beg with a k row, work 14 rows in st st, at the same time, dec 1 st at each end of Rows 5, 7, 9, 11, and 13. (2 sts.)
Bind off.

Sides (Make 1)

With US 9 (5½ mm) needles and 2 strands of Cream, cast on 10 sts.

Beg with a k row, work 52 rows in st st.

Bind off.

BALL (Make 2)

With US 9 (5½ mm) needles and 2 strands of Cream, cast on 14 sts.

K 1 row.

* **Row 2:** Sl 1, p12, turn.

Row 3: K11, turn.

Row 4: P10, turn.

Row 5: K9, turn.

Row 6: P8, turn.

Row 7: K7, turn.

Row 8: P to end. *

Next row: Change to Yellow and k all sts to end.

Rep from * to *

Next row: Change to Pink and k all sts to end.

Rep from * to *

Next row: Change to Blue and k all sts to end.

Rep from * to *

Next row: Change to Turquoise and k all sts to end.

Rep from * to *

Next row: Change to Lilac and k all sts to end.

Rep from * to *

Bind off.

CORDS (Make 4 Short and 2 Long)
Short

With US 9 (5½ mm) needles and 2 strands of Cream, cast on 3 sts.

K 1 row, turn and sl all sts back onto the right needle. Turn again, and pulling the yarn tight from the left side, k across the 3 sts. In this way you will k all rows and the row ends will pull together to make a tube.

Cont in this way until the cord measures 4 cm (1½ in.). Break yarn, thread through sts, draw up tightly and fasten off.

Long

With US 9 (5½ mm) needles and 2 strands of Cream, cast on 3 sts.

K 1 row, turn and sl all sts back onto the right needle. Turn again, and pulling the yarn tight from the left side, k across the 3 sts. In this way you will k all rows and the row ends will pull together to make a tube.

Cont in this way until the cord measures 10 in. (25.5 cm). Break yarn, thread through sts, draw up tightly and fasten off.

FELTING INSTRUCTIONS

Work in all ends with a needle.

Following the instructions on page 17 for hand felting, felt all pieces for approximately 30 minutes. Reshape while damp, and dry thoroughly.

TO MAKE UP
Cubes

Sew short ends of Blue side piece together. Then sew to each Pink face piece leaving an opening. Stuff and close opening.

Repeat with the other pieces using Pink side piece and Blue faces.

Triangle

Sew short ends of side piece together. Then sew to each face piece leaving an opening. Stuff and insert bell if wished, and close opening.

Balls

Gather up each end, then sew seam, leaving an opening. Stuff and close opening.

Sew short cords between the triangle, squares and balls. Sew long cords either side of balls.

Ziggy Zebra

Navy and pale blue stripes offer a twist on traditional zebra colors in this knitted version. Ziggy is bound to become a firm favorite with your little one.

felted knitting

★
☆
☆

SKILL LEVEL:
easy

MEASUREMENTS
Approximately 14 in. (35 cm) tall

MATERIALS
- 2 x 25 g balls of Shetland Wool Brokers 2 ply Jumper Weight in Navy 21
- 2 x 25 g balls of Shetland Wool Brokers 2 ply Jumper Weight in Pale Blue 14
- Pair of US 9 (5½ mm) knitting needles
- Stranded embroidery thread in Black and White
- Washable toy stuffing

ABBREVIATIONS
See page 10.

GAUGE
16 sts and 23 rows to 4 in. (10 cm) measured over stockinette stitch using US 9 (5½ mm) needles and 2 strands of yarn, before hand felting.

Note: Two strands of yarn are used together, throughout, for all pieces.

ZEBRA

BODY FRONT
With US 9 (5½ mm) needles and 2 strands of Navy, cast on 19 sts.
Beg with a k row and working 2 rows Navy, 2 rows Pale Blue throughout, work 26 rows in st st.
* **Next row:** K1, skpo, k to last 3 sts, k2tog, k1.
P 1 row.
Rep last 2 rows once more. (15 sts.)
Bind off. *

BODY BACK
With US 9 (5½ mm) needles and 2 strands of Navy, cast on 19 sts.

Beg with a k row, work 2 rows in st st.
Shape base
Next row: Sl 1, yf, sl 1, yb, k to last 2 sts, yf, sl 1, yb, sl 1.
P 1 row.
Rep the last 2 rows twice more.
Change to Pale Blue. Beg with a k row and working 2 rows Pale Blue, 2 rows Navy throughout, work 20 rows in st st.
Work as for body front from * to *.

ARMS (Make 2)
With US 9 (5½ mm) needles and 2 strands of Pale Blue, cast on 15 sts.
Beg with a k row and working 2 rows Pale Blue, 2 rows Navy throughout, work 18 rows in st st.
Beg with a k row and working in Navy only, work 4 rows in st st.

Next row: K1, skpo, k3, skpo, k4, k2tog, k1. (12 sts.)
P 1 row.
Next row: K1, [k2tog] 5 times, k1. (7 sts.)
P 1 row.
Bind off.

LEGS (Make 2)

With US 9 (5½ mm) needles and 2 strands of Navy, cast on
20 sts.
Beg with a k row work 6 rows in st st.
Change to Pale Blue. Beg with a k row and working 2 rows
Pale Blue, 2 rows Navy throughout, work 24 rows in st st.
Bind off.

LEG BASES (Make 2)

With US 9 (5½ mm) needles and 2 strands of Navy, cast on 4
sts.
Next row: Inc 1 st at each end of row.
P 1 row.
Rep the last 2 rows once more. (8 sts.)
Next row: Dec 1 st at each end of row.
P 1 row.
Rep the last 2 rows once more. (4 sts.)
Bind off.

Above: *head and face detail*

Above: *detail of legs*

HEAD

With US 9 (5½ mm) needles and 2 strands of Navy, cast on
15 sts.
K 1 row.
Next row: [P1, m1] to last 2 sts, p2. (28 sts.)
Change to Pale Blue.
Next row: K8, [m1, k2] 6 times, m1, k8. (35 sts.)
P 1 row.
Cont in 2 rows Navy, 2 rows Pale Blue throughout, work
6 rows in st st.
Next row: K8, skpo, k3, skpo, k1, skpo, k1, k2tog, k3,
k2tog, k9. (30 sts.)
Beg with a p row, and cont in 2 row stripes, work 11 rows in
st st.
Next row: K8, [skpo] twice, k6, [k2tog] twice, k8. (26 sts.)
P 1 row.
Bind off.

MUZZLE

With US 9 (5½ mm) needles and 2 strands of Pale Blue, cast on 30 sts.

Beg with a k row, work 6 rows in st st.

Next row: K7, [skpo] twice, k8, [k2tog] twice, k7. (26 sts.)

P 1 row.

Next row: K5, [skpo] 3 times, k4, [k2tog] 3 times, k5. (20 sts.)

P 1 row.

Next row: K1, [k2tog] to last st, k1. (11 sts.)

P 1 row.

Bind off.

EARS (Make 2)

With US 9 (5½ mm) needles and 2 strands of Pale Blue, cast on 5 sts.

Beg with a k row, work 4 rows in st st.

Next row: Skpo, k1, k2tog. (3 sts.)

Change to Navy.

P 1 row.

Next row: [K1, m1] twice, k1. (5 sts.)

Beg with a p row, work 7 rows in st st.

Bind off.

TAIL

With US 9 (5½ mm) needles and 2 strands of Navy, cast on 3 sts.

K 1 row, turn and sl all sts back onto the right needle.

Turn again, and pulling the yarn tight from the left side,

k across the 3 sts. In this way you will k all rows and the row ends will pull together to make a tube.

Cont in this way until the tail measures 4 in. (10 cm).

Bind off.

Loop 6 x 3 in. (8 cm) lengths of Navy yarn through one end of tail.

FELTING INSTRUCTIONS

Work in all ends with a needle.

Following the instructions on page 17 for hand felting, felt all pieces for approximately 20 minutes.

Reshape while damp, and dry thoroughly.

TO MAKE UP

Join each inside leg seam and stitch to each leg base. Stuff firmly and oversew cast-off edges together.

Sew underarm seam of each arm and stuff firmly. Oversew cast-on edges together.

Above: *when felting the tail, roll the cord between your hands to mat well*

Pin oversewn edges of legs to lower front body and one arm to side of front body. Sew front body to back body through all thicknesses, leaving one side open. Turn to right side, attach other arm and close side seam.

Stuff firmly and close top seam.

Sew tail to center of broad Navy section on back body.

Sew center back seam of head.

Fold each ear in half and sew row-ends together.

Pin ears inside top seam of head and sew through all thicknesses to close.

Stuff head firmly.

Join seam of muzzle and stuff. Sew muzzle to front of head, positioning over shaping.

Sew head to shoulders.

Stitch eyes and nostrils in satin stitch using black embroidery thread. Work mouth in black embroidery thread using stem stitch. Sew a small white highlight in each eye.

Cool Cat

Knitted in a wonderful tweed yarn that felts beautifully, here's a cuddly, cool cat waiting to be a cute companion.

MEASUREMENTS
Approximately 11 in. (28 cm) tall

MATERIALS
- 2 x 25 g balls of Rowan Scottish Tweed 4 ply in Orange/Sunset 11
- 1 x 25 g ball of Rowan Scottish Tweed 4 ply in Dark Red/Lobster 17
- 1 x 25 g ball of Rowan Scottish Tweed 4 ply in Light Brown/Rust 9
- 1 x 25 g ball of Rowan Scottish Tweed 4 ply in Dark Brown/Peat 19
- Pair of US 9 (5½ mm) knitting needles
- Stranded embroidery thread in Black and White
- Washable toy stuffing

ABBREVIATIONS
See page 10.

GAUGE
16 sts and 22 rows to 4 in. (10 cm) measured over stockinette stitch using US 9 (5½ mm) needles and 2 strands of yarn, before hand felting.

Note: Two strands of yarn are used together, throughout, for all pieces.

CAT

BODY
Right leg
* With US 9 (5½ mm) needles and 2 strands of Orange, cast on 10 sts.
Next row: Inc 1 st, k wise, in every st. (20 sts.)
Beg with a p row, work 19 rows in st st.*
Break yarn and place sts on a spare needle.
Left leg
Work as for right leg from * to *.
Join legs
With RS facing and 2 strands of Dark Red, k across 20 sts of Left leg, then 20 sts of right leg. (40 sts.)
Next row: P20, m1, p20. (41 sts.)
Beg with a k row and working 2 rows Orange, 2 rows Light Brown, 2 rows Dark Brown and 2 rows Dark Red throughout, work 28 rows in st st.
Shape shoulders
Cont stripe sequence as set, work as follows:
Next row: K9, skpo, k19, k2tog, k9. (39 sts.)
P 1 row.
Next row: K2, [k2tog, k1] to last 4 sts, k2tog, k2. (27 sts.)
P 1 row.
Bind off.

HEAD (Make 2)

With US 9 (5½ mm) needles and 2 strands of Orange, cast on 6 sts.

K 1 row.

Cast on 2 sts at beg of next 4 rows. (14 sts.)

P 1 row.

Inc 1 st at each end of next and foll alt row. (18 sts.)

Beg with a p row, work 11 rows in st st.

Divide for ears

Next row: K5, bind off 8 sts, k5.

Working on these 5 sts only as follows:

Next row: P3, p2tog. (4 sts.)

Next row: K2tog, k2. (3 sts.)

Next row: P1, p2tog. (2 sts.)

Next row: K2tog.

Break yarn, thread through rem st and fasten off.

With WS facing, rejoin yarn to rem 5 sts and work as for first ear, reversing all shapings.

ARMS (Make 2)

With US 9 (5½ mm) needles and 2 strands of Orange, cast on 8 sts.

Next row: Inc 1 st, k wise, in every st. (16 sts.)

Beg with a p row, work 19 rows in st st.

Shape top

Beg with a k row, work 6 rows in st st, dec 1 st at each end of every row. (4 sts.)

Bind off.

TAIL

With US 9 (5½ mm) needles and 2 strands of Orange, cast on 4 sts.

K 1 row, turn and sl all sts back onto the right needle.

Turn again, and pulling the yarn tight from the left side, k across the 4 sts. In this way you will k all rows and the row-ends will pull together to make tube.

Cont in this way until the tail measures 4 in. (10 cm).

Break yarn, thread through sts, draw up tightly and fasten off.

FELTING INSTRUCTIONS

Work in all ends with a needle.

Following the instructions on page 17 for hand felting, felt all pieces for approximately 25 minutes.

Reshape while damp, and dry thoroughly.

TO MAKE UP

Sew each inside leg seam. Then sew the center back seam catching the tail into the seam just above the tops of the legs. Stuff and close top opening.

With right sides together, sew the two head pieces together, leaving an opening. Turn to right side, stuff firmly and close opening.

Sew head to body.

Sew bottom and underarm seam of each arm. Stuff and sew to sides of body.

Work eyes and nose in satin stitch using black embroidery thread. Work mouth and whiskers in stem stitch and black embroidery thread. Sew a small white highlight in each eye. Using black embroidery thread, work 'claws' on hands and feet in stem stitch.

Left: *roll the tail between your hands when felting to produce a good effect*

Stig Steg

The yarn used to knit this dinosaur is a wonderful lofty, random dyed one which perfectly evokes scales. Because the yarn is so thick it knits up really quickly, making it perfect for a beginner.

plain knitting

★
☆
☆

SKILL LEVEL: **easy**

MEASUREMENTS
Approximately 11 in. (28 cm) long

MATERIALS
- 1 x 100 g ball of Rowan Spray in Green/Landscape
- Small amount of Rowan Spray in Multi/Sensation
- Pair of US 11 (8 mm) knitting needles
- Stranded embroidery thread in Black and White
- Washable toy stuffing

ABBREVIATIONS
See page 10.

GAUGE
10 sts and 14 rows to 4 in. (10 cm) measured over reverse stockinette stitch using US 11 (8 mm) needles.

DINOSAUR

RIGHT SIDE

With US 11 (8 mm) needles and Green, cast on 3 sts.
Beg with a k row, work 7 rows in st st.
Next row: P to last st, inc 1. (4 sts.)
Beg with a k row, work 2 rows in st st.
Next row: K, inc 1 st at each end of row. (6 sts.)
Shape back leg
Next row: Cast on 4 sts, p to end. (10 sts.)
Beg with a k row, work 5 rows in st st, at the same time, inc 1 st at beg of Rows 1, 3 and 5. (13 sts.)
Next row: Bind off 4 sts, p to end. (9 sts.)
Beg with a k row, work 5 rows in st st, at the same time, inc 1 st at beg of Rows 1, 3 and 5. (12 sts.)
Shape front leg
Next row: Cast on 4 sts, p to end. (16 sts.)
Beg with a k row, work 5 rows in st st, at the same time,

dec 1 st at beg of Rows 1, 3 and 5. (13 sts.)
Next row: Bind off 5 sts, p to end. (8 sts.)
Shape head
Beg with a k row, work 2 rows in st st.
Next row: [K2tog] twice, k to last st, inc in last st. (7 sts.)
P 1 row.
Next row: K2tog, k to last st, inc in last st. (7 sts.)
P 1 row.
Next row: K2tog, k to end. (6 sts.)
Beg with a p row, work 3 rows in st st.
Next row: K2tog, k2, k2tog. (4 sts.)
P 1 row.
Bind off.

LEFT SIDE

With US 11 (8 mm) needles and Green, cast on 3 sts.
Beg with a k row, work 7 rows in st st.
Next row: Inc 1, p to end. (4 sts.)
K 1 row.

Next row: P, inc 1 st at each end of row. (6 sts.)

Shape back leg

Next row: Cast on 4 sts, k to end. (10 sts.)

Beg with a p row, work 5 rows in st st, at the same time, inc 1 st at beg of Rows 1, 3 and 5. (13 sts.)

Next row: Bind off 4 sts, k to end. (9 sts.)

Beg with a p row, work 5 rows in st st, at the same time, inc 1 st at beg of Rows 1, 3 and 5. (12 sts.)

Shape front leg

Next row: Cast on 4 sts, k to end. (16 sts.)

Beg with a p row, work 5 rows in st st, at the same time, sdec 1 st at beg of Rows 1, 3 and 5. (13 sts.)

Next row: Bind off 5 sts, k to end. (8 sts.)

Shape head

Beg with a p row, work 2 rows in st st.

Next row: [P2tog] twice, p to last st, inc in last st. (7 sts.)

K 1 row.

Next row: P2tog, p to last st, inc in last st. (7 sts.)

K 1 row.

Next row: P2tog, p to end. (6 sts.)

Beg with a k row, work 3 rows in st st.

Next row: P2tog, p2, p2tog. (4 sts.)

K 1 row.

Bind off.

GUSSET

With US 11 (8 mm) needles and Green, cast on 2 sts.

Beg with a k row, work 2 rows in st st.

Next row: Inc 1 st at each end of row. (4 sts.)

Shape back leg

Next row: Cast on 4 sts, p to end. (8 sts.)

Next row: Cast on 4 sts, k to end. (12 sts.)

Beg with a p row, work 4 rows in st st.

Next row: Bind off 4 sts, p to end. (8 sts.)

Next row: Bind off 4 sts, k to end. (4 sts.)

Beg with a p row, work 6 rows in st st.

Shape front leg

Next row: Cast on 4 sts, p to end. (8 sts.)

Next row: Cast on 4 sts, k to end. (12 sts.)

Beg with a p row, work 4 rows in st st.

Next row: Bind off 5 sts, p to end. (7 sts.)

Next row: Bind off 5 sts, k to end. (2 sts.)

Beg with a p row, work 3 rows in st st.

Bind off.

POINTS

With US 11 (8 mm) needles and Multi, cast on 28 sts.

K 2 rows.

Working in g st throughout, cont as follows.

* **Next row:** K2, turn.

Next row: K2.

Next row: K2tog.

Break yarn, thread through rem st, pull tightly and fasten off.*

With RS facing rejoin yarn to rem sts and rep from * to * once more.

With RS facing rejoin yarn to rem sts and cont as follows:

** **Next row:** K3, turn.

Next row: K3.

Next row: K2tog, k1.

Next row: K2tog.

Break yarn, thread through rem st, pull tightly and fasten off. **

With RS facing rejoin yarn to rem sts and cont as follows:

*** **Next row:** K4, turn.

Next row: K4.

Next row: [K2tog] twice.

Next row: K2tog.

Break yarn, thread through rem st, pull tightly and fasten off. ***

With RS facing rejoin yarn to rem sts and rep from *** to *** 3 times.

With RS facing rejoin yarn to rem sts and rep from ** to ** once.

With RS facing rejoin yarn to rem 2 sts and rep from * to *.

TO MAKE UP

Note: Purl side is right side.

Oversew body sides together catching in points along center back.

Sew gusset to lower edges, leaving an opening. Stuff and close opening.

Embroider eyes in satin stitch using black embroidery thread. Work mouth in stem stitch using black embroidery thread. Use white to stitch highlights and edges of eyes.

Below: *the points are positioned along the back*

Stripes the Tiger

A little jungle friend for your wild one! This striped tiger would look wonderful lying on a child's bed, and the 100% Alpaca yarn is lovely to cuddle up to.

felted knitting

★
★
☆

SKILL LEVEL:
moderate

MEASUREMENTS
Approximately 11 in. (28 cm) long

MATERIALS
- 1 x 50 g ball of Alpaca Select 100% Alpaca DK in Orange 19
- 1 x 50 g ball of Alpaca Select 100% Alpaca DK in Black 9
- Pair of US 7 (4½ mm) knitting needles
- Stranded embroidery thread in Black and White
- Washable toy stuffing

ABBREVIATIONS
See page 10.

GAUGE
20 sts and 25 rows to 4 in. (10 cm) measured over stockinette stitch using US 7 (4½ mm) needles before hand felting.

TIGER

BODY
First front leg

* With US 7 (4½ mm) needles and Orange, cast on 19 sts.

Beg with a k row, work 2 rows in st st.

Next row: K1, m1, k8, m1, k1, m1, k8, m1, k1. (23 sts.)

Beg with a p row, work 7 rows in st st.

Change to Black, and working in stripes of 2 rows Black, 4 rows Orange throughout, cont as follows:

Beg with a k row, work 10 rows in st st. *

Break yarn and place sts on a spare needle.

Second front leg
Work as first front leg from * to *.

Join legs
With US 7 (4½ mm) needles and Orange, and RS facing, k across 23 sts of second front leg, then 23 sts of first front leg.

(46 sts.)

Next row: P22, [m1, p1] 3 times, p21. (49 sts.)

Change to Black and stripe sequence as set, beg with a k row, work 40 rows in st st.

Divide for back legs
Next row: K23, bind off 3 sts, k to end.

First back leg
**Working on these 23 sts, and stripe sequence as set, cont as follows:

Beg with a p row, work 9 rows in st st.

Change to Orange, cont in Orange only, and beg with a k row, work 8 rows in st st.

Next row: K1, k2tog, k7, [k2tog] twice, k6, k2tog, k1.

(19 sts.)

P 1 row.

Bind off. **

Second back leg
With WS facing, rejoin yarn to rem sts and rep from ** to **.

HEAD (Make 2)

With US 7 (4½ mm) needles and Orange, cast on 8 sts.

Working in stripes of 4 rows Orange, 2 rows Black, cont as follows.

Beg with a k row, work 2 rows in st st.

Cast on 2 sts at beg of next 7 rows. (22 sts.)

Beg with a p row, work 13 rows in st st.

Shape ears

Next row: K5, bind off 12 sts, k5.

First ear

Work on these 5 sts only and stripe sequence, cont as follows:

P 1 row.

Next row: K2tog, k to end. (4 sts.)

Next row: P2, p2tog. (3 sts.)

Next row: K2tog, k1. (2 sts.)

Next row: P2tog.

Break yarn, thread through rem st, draw up tightly and fasten off.

Second ear

With WS facing, rejoin yarn to rem sts and work as for first ear, reversing all shaping.

FACE

With US 7 (4½ mm) needles and Orange, cast on 7 sts.

Beg with a k row, work 2 rows in st st.

Below: *back legs and tail detail*

Then, beg with a k row, work 4 rows in st st, inc 1 st at each end of every row. (15 sts.)

Now, beg with a k row, work 6 rows in st st.

Next row: K2tog, k4, k2tog, turn. (6 sts.)

Next row: P2tog, p2, p2tog. (4 sts.)

Bind off.

With RS facing, rejoin yarn to rem 7 sts and work as follows:

Next row: K2tog, k to end. (6 sts.)

Next row: P2tog, p2, p2tog. (4 sts.)

Bind off.

TAIL

With US 7 (4½ mm) needles and Orange, cast on 7 sts.

Beg with a k row and working stripes of 4 rows Orange, 2 rows Black, work 22 rows in st st.

Bind off.

FELTING INSTRUCTIONS

Work in all ends with a needle.

Following the instructions on page 17 for hand felting, felt all pieces for approximately 30 minutes.

Reshape while damp, and dry thoroughly.

TO MAKE UP

Sew each inside leg seam, then the center body seam, leaving an opening for stuffing.

Stuff legs and body firmly and close opening.

Fold tail in half lengthways and join one end and long seam. Stuff lightly. Sew to back just above back legs.

Sew head pieces together, leaving an opening for stuffing. Stuff firmly and close opening. Sew face to front head. Sew head to body.

Embroider eyes and nose in satin stitch using black embroidery thread. Embroider mouth in stem stitch using black. Sew a small white highlight in each eye.

Sew 'claws' on each paw in stem stitch using black embroidery thread.

Maisie Moo

Who says that cows have to be black and white? This fun green and yellow version is sure to raise a smile in all who see her.

felted knitting

★
★
☆

**SKILL LEVEL:
moderate**

MEASUREMENTS
Approximately 12 in. (30 cm) tall

MATERIALS
- 2 x 50 g balls of Alpaca Select 100% Alpaca DK in Yellow 21
- 1 x 50 g ball of Alpaca Select 100% Alpaca DK in Green 23
- 1 x 50 g ball of Alpaca Select 100% Alpaca DK in Pink 37
- Pair of US 7 (4½ mm) knitting needles
- Stranded embroidery thread in Black and White
- Washable toy stuffing

ABBREVIATIONS
See page 10.

GAUGE
20 sts and 25 rows to 4 in. (10 cm) measured over stockinette stitch using US 7 (4½ mm) needles before hand felting.

COW

BODY (Make 2)
With US 7 (4½ mm) needles and Yellow, cast on 28 sts.
Beg with a k row, work 2 rows in st st.
Using the intarsia method, cont as follows:
Row 3: K1, m1, k4 Yellow, 13 Green, 9 Yellow, m1, k1. (30 sts.)
Row 4: P11 Yellow, 13 Green, 6 Yellow.
Row 5: K6 Yellow, 12 Green, 12 Yellow.
Row 6: With Green, P1, m1, p3 Green, 8 Yellow, 11 Green, 6 Yellow, with Green m1, p1. (32 sts.)
Row 7: K3 Green, 6 Yellow, 9 Green, 7 Yellow, 7 Green.
Row 8: P8 Green, 7 Yellow, 7 Green, 6 Yellow, 4 Green.
Row 9: K1, m1, k4 Green, 6 Yellow, 6 Green, 7 Yellow, 7 Green, m1, k1. (34 sts.)

Row 10: P10 Green, 7 Yellow, 4 Green, 6 Yellow, 7 Green.
Row 11: K7 Green, 16 Yellow, 11 Green.
Row 12: P12 Green, 14 Yellow, 8 Green.
Row 13: K8 Green, 13 Yellow, 13 Green.
Row 14: P13 Green, 13 Yellow, 8 Green.
Row 15: K8 Green, 12 Yellow, 14 Green.
Row 16: P14 Green, 12 Yellow, 8 Green.
Row 17: As Row 15.
Row 18: As Row 16.
Row 19: K2tog, k6 Green, 13 Yellow, 11 Green, k2tog. (32 sts.)
Row 20: P11 Green, 14 Yellow, 7 Green.
Row 21: K7 Green, 14 Yellow, 11 Green.
Row 22: As Row 20.
Row 23: As Row 21.
Row 24: P10 Green, 5 Yellow, 3 Green, 7 Yellow, 7 Green.
Row 25: K6 Green, 7 Yellow, 5 Green, 4 Yellow, 10 Green.

Row 26: P9 Green, 5 Yellow, 6 Green, 6 Yellow, 6 Green.

Row 27: K2tog, k4 Green, 6 Yellow, 7 Green, 4 Yellow, 7 Green, k2tog. (30 sts.)

Row 28: P6 Green, 6 Yellow, 8 Green, 6 Yellow, 4 Green.

Row 29: K2 Green, 8 Yellow, 9 Green, 8 Yellow, 3 Green.

Row 30: With Yellow, p2tog, p9 Yellow, 9 Green, 8 Yellow, p2tog. (28 sts.)

Row 31: K9 Yellow, 9 Green, 10 Yellow.

Row 32: P10 Yellow, 9 Green, 9 Yellow.

Row 33: K2tog, k8 Yellow, 8 Green, 8 Yellow, k2tog. (26 sts.)

Row 34: P10 Yellow, 6 Green, 10 Yellow.

Row 35: K2tog, k9 Yellow, 4 Green, 9 Yellow, k2tog. (24 sts.)

Row 36: P all sts in Yellow.

Row 37: K2tog, k to last 2 sts, k2tog. (22 sts.)

Row 38: P2tog, p to last 2 sts, p2tog. (20 sts.)

K 1 row.

Row 40: P2tog, p to last 2 sts, p2tog. (18 sts.)

Beg with a k row, work 2 rows in st st.

Bind off.

BODY BASE

With US 7 (4½ mm) needles and Yellow, cast on 9 sts.

Beg with a k row, work 2 rows in st st.

Cast on 4 sts at beg of next 4 rows. (25 sts.)

Beg with a k row, work 2 rows in st st.

Bind off 4 sts at beg of next 4 rows. (9 sts.)

Beg with a k row, work 2 rows in st st.

Bind off.

ARMS (Make 2)

With US 7 (4½ mm) needles and Yellow, cast on 19 sts.

Working from Chart A, work 22 rows in st st.

Bind off.

Above: *detail of Maisie Moo's face*

ARM HOOVES (Make 2)

With US 7 (4½ mm) needles and Pink, cast on 7 sts.

Beg with a k row, work 8 rows in st st.

Bind off.

LEGS (Make 2)

With US 7 (4½ mm) needles and Yellow, cast on 27 sts.

Working from Chart B, work 20 rows in st st.

Bind off.

KEY

☐ Yellow

 Green

CHART A

CHART B

LEG HOOVES (Make 2)

With US 7 (4½ mm) needles and Pink, cast on 9 sts.
Beg with a k row, work 2 rows in st st.
Work 6 rows in st st, dec 1 st at each end of every alt row.
(3 sts.)
Bind off.

HEAD

With US 7 (4½ mm) needles and Yellow, cast on 39 sts.
Beg with a k row, work 2 rows in st st.
Next row: K10, [m1, k2] 10 times, k9. (49 sts.)
Beg with a p row, work 7 rows in st st.
Next row: K10, [k2tog, k1] 10 times, k9. (39 sts.)
Beg with a p row, work 11 rows in st st.
Next row: K2, [k2tog, k1] to last 4 sts, k2tog, k2. (27 sts.)
Next row: P1, [p2tog] to end. (14 sts.)
Bind off.

NOSE

With US 7 (4½ mm) needles and Pink, cast on 50 sts.
Beg with a k row, work 8 rows in st st.
Next row: K3, [k2tog, k4] to last 5 sts, k2tog, k3. (42 sts.)
P 1 row.
Next row: K2, [k2tog, k3] to end. (34 sts.)
P 1 row.
Next row: K1, [k2tog, k1] to end. (23 sts.)
P 1 row.
Bind off.

EARS (Make 2)

With US 7 (4½ mm) needles and Green, cast on 6 sts.
Beg with a k row, work 6 rows in st st.
Next row: Skpo, k2, k2tog. (4 sts.)
P 1 row.
Next row: K1, m1, k2, m1, k1. (6 sts.)
Beg with a p row, work 7 rows in st st.
Bind off.

HORNS (Make 2)

With US 7 (4½ mm) needles and Pink, cast on 8 sts.
Beg with a k row, work 6 rows in st st, at the same time dec
1 st at each end of every alt row. (2 sts)
Work 2 rows in st st.
Bind off.

FELTING INSTRUCTIONS

Work in all ends with a needle.

Following the instructions on page 17 for hand felting, felt all
pieces for approximately 30 minutes.
Reshape while damp, and dry thoroughly.

TO MAKE UP

Stitch body pieces together at sides.
Sew leg seams. With cast-off edge of hoof to leg seam, sew
hooves into cast-on ends of legs. Stuff and oversew ends.
Sew body base into bottom of body, sewing tops of legs into
front of seam.
Stuff body and close seam.
Sew top and center back seam of head and stuff.
Sew row-ends of nose together. With seam at center, sew
cast-off edges together. Stuff and sew to head over front
shaping and bottom edges.
Sew horn seams and stuff. Oversew bottom edges. Sew
row-ends of ears together and oversew bottom edges. Sew
horns and ears to top of head.
Sew head to body.
Sew arm seams, then sew hooves in cast-off ends. Stuff,
oversew ends then sew to sides of body.
Embroider eyes and nostrils in satin stitch using black
embroidery thread. Sew a small white highlight in each eye.

Above: *when making up the horns, curve and mold them
to achieve the correct shape*

Poppy Pig

A sweet piglet knitted entirely in garter stitch makes for a wonderfully soft little friend. Her fun hat and scarf add to the cuteness factor.

plain knitting

SKILL LEVEL:
moderate

MEASUREMENTS
Approximately 10 in. (25 cm) tall

MATERIALS
- 2 x 50 g balls of Rowan Calmer in Pink/Powder Puff 482
- 1 x 50 g ball of Rowan Calmer in Bright Pink/Blush 477
- 1 x 50 g ball of Rowan Calmer in Green/Kiwi 485
- 1 x 50 g ball of Rowan Calmer in Blue/Refresh 487
- Pair of US 6 (4 mm) knitting needles
- Stranded embroidery thread in Black and White
- Washable toy stuffing

ABBREVIATIONS
See page 10.

GAUGE
Big Value Baby DK
24 sts and 44 rows to 4 in. (10 cm) measured over garter stitch using US 6 (4 mm) needles.
24 sts and 34 rows to 4 in. (10 cm) measured over stockinette stitch using US 6 (4 mm) needles.

PIG

BODY FRONT

With US 6 (4 mm) needles and Pink, cast on 34 sts.
*Work in g st throughout.
K 24 rows.
Then K 36 rows, at the same time, dec 1 st at each end of every foll 4th row. * (16 sts.)
Bind off.

BODY BACK

With US 6 (4 mm) needles and Pink, cast on 36 sts.
Work as for Body Front from * to *. (18 sts.)
Bind off.

BODY BASE

With US 6 (4 mm) needles and Pink, cast on 10 sts.
Work in g st throughout.
Cast on 2 sts at beg of next 2 rows. (14 sts.)
Inc 1 st at each end of next 7 rows. (28 sts.)
K 4 rows.
Dec 1 st at each end of next 7 rows. (14 sts.)
Bind off 2 sts at beg of next 2 rows. (10 sts.)
Bind off.

HEAD (Make 2)

With US 6 (4 mm) needles and Pink, cast on 5 sts.
Work in g st throughout.
Inc 1 st at each end of the next 4 rows. (13 sts.)
Now k 6 rows, inc 1 st at each end of every alt row. (19 sts.)

Then k 6 rows, inc 1 st at each end of every 3rd row. (23 sts.)
K 4 rows straight.
Now k 8 rows, inc 1 st at each end of every 4th row. (27sts)
K 6 rows straight.
Then k 9 rows, dec 1 st at each end of every row. (9 sts.)
K 1 row.
Bind off.

SNOUT

With US 6 (4 mm) needles and Pink, cast on 4 sts.
Work in g st throughout.
Cast on 2 sts at beg of next 2 rows. (8 sts.)
K 1 row.
Next row: Inc 1 st at each end of row. (10 sts.)
K 8 rows.
Next row: Dec 1 st at each end of row. (8 sts.)
K 1 row.
Bind off 2 sts at beg of next 2 rows. (4 sts.)
Bind off.

SNOUT SIDE

With US 6 (4 mm) needles and Pink, cast on 4 sts.
Work in g st throughout.
K until work measures 13 cm (5 in.).
Bind off.

EARS (Make 2)

With US 6 (4 mm) needles and Pink, cast on 6 sts.
Work in g st throughout.
K 8 rows, inc 1 st at each end of every 4th row. (10 sts.)
K 4 rows.
Then k 4 rows, dec 1 st at each end of 4th row. (8 sts.)
K 6 rows, dec 1 st at each end of every alt row. (2 sts.)
K 1 row.
K2tog.
Break yarn and pull through rem st.

ARMS (Make 2)

With US 6 (4 mm) needles and Pink, cast on 4 sts.
K 2 rows.
Next row: K1, m1, k to last st, m1, k1. (6 sts.)
K 1 row.
Rep the last 2 rows until there are 18 sts.
K 20 rows.
Next row: K1, [k2tog] to last st, k1. (10 sts.)
Next row: [K2tog] 5 times. (5 sts.)
Break yarn, thread through rem 5 sts and draw up tightly.

LEGS (Make 2)

With US 6 (4 mm) needles and Pink, cast on 20 sts.
Work in g st throughout.
Next row: K4, m1, k to last 4 sts, m1, k4. (22 sts.)
K 1 row.
Rep the last 2 rows until there are 38 sts.
K 4 rows straight.
Bind off.

HOOVES (Make 2)

With US 6 (4 mm) needles and Pink, cast on 4 sts.
Work in g st throughout.
K 2 rows.
Then k 12 rows, inc 1 st at each end of every 4th row.
(10 sts.)
K 2 rows.
Shape toes
Next row: K 5, turn.
Work on these sts only, as follows:
K 2 rows.
Next row: K2tog, k to end. (4 sts.)
K 1 row.
Next row: [K2tog] twice. (2 sts.)
K 1 row.
Bind off.
Rejoin yarn to rem sts and complete as for first toe, making
first dec at inside edge of toe.

TAIL

With US 6 (4 mm) needles and Pink, cast on 8 sts.
Next row: Inc k wise in every st. (16 sts.)
K 1 row.
Bind off loosely.

TO MAKE UP

Join side seams of body pieces. Sew body base to lower
edges of body pieces. Stuff through top opening and then
close seam. Fold each leg piece in half and sew short ends
together. Sew each hoof into the broad end of each leg,
lining up the increase line with the points of the toes. Stuff
lightly and oversew top edges together. Stitch to body
placing oversewn edge on the seam line formed where the
body meets the body base. Sew head pieces together
catching in ears in the top seam and leaving an opening.
Stuff and close opening. Sew head to body. Sew the cast-on
and cast-off edges of the snout side together. Sew the snout
side to the snout and stuff lightly. Sew to face. Catch the

points of the ears forward onto the ears to form a fold.
Sew each arm seam and stuff. Sew each arm to sides of
body. Twist tail to form a spiral and stitch to back of body.
Embroider eyes and nostrils in satin stitch, using black.

Above: *back detail showing tail*

Embroider mouth in stem stitch, using black. Sew a small
white highlight in each eye.

CLOTHES

HAT

With US 6 (4 mm) needles and Bright Pink, cast on
40 sts.

Beg with a k row, work 4 rows in st st.

Next row: [P7, k1] 5 times.

Next row: [P1, k7] 5 times.

Rep the last 2 rows 3 times more.

Next row: [P1, [p2tog] 3 times, k1] to end. (25 sts.)

Next row: [P1, [k2tog] twice] to end. (15 sts.)

Next row: [P2tog, k1] to end. (10 sts.)

Next row: [P2tog] to end. (5 sts.)

Break yarn (leaving a long length for making up), thread
through rem 5 sts and draw up tightly.

TO MAKE UP

Using the yarn at the top of the hat, and right sides together,
sew seam, reversing the seam for the 4 rows of stockinette
stitch at the bottom as this will curl back. Make a pom-pom
in Blue, approximately 1¼ in. (3 cm) in diameter, and attach
to top of hat. If desired, stitch hat to top of pig's head.

SCARF

With US 6 (4 mm) needles and Bright Pink, cast on
10 sts.

Beg with a k row, and working in st st stripes of 4 rows
Bright Pink, 4 rows Blue, 4 rows Green throughout, work
until scarf measures 14 in. (35 cm) long.

Bind off.

TO MAKE UP

Make two pom-poms in Blue, approximately 1¼ in. (3 cm)
in diameter. Gather up each end of the scarf and attach a
pom-pom to each end. Tie around pig's neck.

Above: *Poppy Pig's hat with pom-pom*

Above: *the scarf with pom-pom ends*

Chilly Billy

A happy chap in his hat and scarf; Chilly Billy would make a lovely gift for a toddler or new baby. The stark contrasts of a penguin's colors are known to stimulate new babies' vision.

plain knitting

SKILL LEVEL:
moderate

MEASUREMENTS
Approximately 9 in. (23 cm) tall

MATERIALS
- 1 x 50 g ball of Jaeger Matchmaker Merino DK in Black 681
- 1 x 50 g ball of Jaeger Matchmaker Merino DK in White 661
- 1 x 50 g ball of Jaeger Matchmaker Merino DK in Orange/Pumpkin 898
- Small amounts of Jaeger Matchmaker Merino DK in Red/Cherry 656 and Pink/Rock Rose 896
- Pair US 3 (3¼ mm) knitting needles
- Stranded embroidery thread in Black and White
- Washable toy stuffing

ABBREVIATIONS
See page 10.

GAUGE
Big Value Baby DK
26 sts and 34 rows to 10 cm (4 in.) measured over stockinette stitch using 3¼ mm (UK 10/US 3) needles.

PENGUIN

BODY & HEAD
With US 3 (3¼ mm) needles and Black, cast on 62 sts.
Beg with a k row, work 2 rows in st st.
Next row: K6, [m1, k10] 5 times, m1, k6. (68 sts.)
Beg with a p row, work 27 rows in st st.

Shape for head
Next row: K6, [k2tog, k16] 3 times, k2tog, k6. (64 sts.)
P 1 row.
Next row: K6, [k2tog, k15] 3 times, k2tog, k5. (60 sts.)
P 1 row.
Next row: K5, [k2tog, k14] 3 times, k2tog, k5. (56 sts.)
P 1 row.
Next row: K6, [k2tog, k12] 3 times, k2tog, k6. (52 sts.)

P 1 row.
Next row: K7, [k2tog, k10] 3 times, k2tog, k7. (48 sts.)
P 1 row.
Next row: K3, [k2tog, k6] 5 times, k2tog, k3. (42 sts.)
Beg with a p row, work 23 rows in st st.

Shape top of head
Next row: K3, [k2tog, k3] 7 times, k2tog, k2. (34 sts.)
P 1 row.
Next row: K2, [k2tog, k2] 8 times. (26 sts.)
P 1 row.
Next row: K2, [k2tog, k1] 8 times. (18 sts.)
P 1 row.
Next row: K1, [k2tog, k1] 5 times, k2tog. (12 sts.)
Next row: [P2tog] to end. (6 sts.)
Break yarn (leaving a long length for making up), thread through remaining 6 sts and draw up tightly.

Above: *the penguin looks snug in his hat and scarf*

BODY BASE

With US 3 (3¼ mm) needles and Black, cast on
10 sts.
Beg with a k row, work 2 rows in st st.
Cast on 2 sts at beg of next 6 rows. (22 sts.)
Beg with a k row, work 6 rows in st st.
Bind off 2 sts at beg of next 6 rows. (10 sts.)
Beg with a k row, work 2 rows in st st.
Bind off.

CHEST

With US 3 (3¼ mm) needles and White, cast on
15 sts.
Beg with a k row, work 26 rows in st st.
Shape top
Next row: K1, skpo, k to last 3 sts, k2tog, k1.
P 1 row.
Rep last 2 rows once more. (11 sts.)
Next row: K1, skpo, k to last 3 sts, k2tog, k1. (9 sts.)
Bind off 2 sts at beg of next 3 rows. (3 sts.)
Bind off.

WINGS (Make 4)

With US 3 (3¼ mm) needles and Black, cast on 7 sts.
Beg with a k row, work 2 rows in st st.
Next row: K1, m1, k to last st, m1, k1.
P 1 row.
Rep the last 2 rows until there are 13 sts.
Beg with a k row, work 14 rows in st st.

Beg with a k row, work 12 rows, dec 1 st at each end of every
foll 4th row. (7 sts.)
Beg with a k row, work 2 rows in st st.
Bind off 2 sts at beg of next 2 rows. (3 sts.)
Bind off.

FEET (Make 2)

With US 3 (3¼ mm) needles and Orange, cast on 8 sts.
Beg with a k row, work 2 rows in st st.
Beg with a k row, work 5 rows in st st, inc 1 st at each end
of next and every foll k row. (14 sts.)
Beg with a p row, work 23 rows in st st.
Beg with a k row, work 6 rows in st st, dec 1 st at each end
of next and every foll k row. (8 sts.)
Bind off.

BEAK

With US 3 (3¼ mm) needles and Orange, cast on 5 sts.
Beg with a k row, work 2 rows in st st.
Next row: Skpo, k1, k2tog. (3 sts.)
Next row: P2tog, p1. (2 sts.)
Next row: K2tog. (1 st.)
Next row: P, inc into st. (2 sts.)
Next row: Inc into 1st st, k1. (3 sts.)
Next row: Inc into 1st st, p2. (4 sts.)
Next row: Inc into 1st st, k3. (5 sts.)
P 1 row.
Bind off.

TO MAKE UP

Sew center back seam of body.
Fold each foot in half and sew down each side. Stuff lightly
and oversew cast-on and cast-off edges together. Sew two,
evenly spaced, lines through all thicknesses to form toes.
Pin oversewn edges of feet to front lower edge of body.
Pin body base over feet, sew through all thicknesses,
gathering back bottom edge slightly to fit, and leaving an
opening. Stuff firmly and close opening.
Sew chest to front of body.
Sew two wing pieces together for each wing, and then sew
to sides of body.
Fold beak in half and sew row-ends together. Stitch to face.
Sew eyes in satin stitch using white embroidery thread. Then
sew pupil in each eye with black thread. Sew a small white
highlight in each eye.

CLOTHES

SCARF

With US 3 (3¼ mm) needles and Pink, cast on 6 sts and work in g st as follows:
K 2 rows Pink, k 2 rows Red and k 2 rows Orange.
These 6 rows form patt rep. Cont in stripe patt until scarf measures 12 in. (30 cm).
Bind off.

Fringing

Cut 4 x 3 in. (8 cm) lengths each of Pink, Red and Orange. Following the fringing instructions on page 15, knot through each end of the scarf as per the photograph.

HAT

With US 3 (3¼ mm) needles and Pink, cast on 46 sts.
Beg with a k row, work 16 rows in st st, working 2 rows Pink, 2 rows Red, 2 rows Orange throughout.

Shape top

The foll 4 rows are all worked in Orange.
Next row: K1, [k2tog] to last st, k1. (24 sts.)
P 1 row.
Next row: [K2tog] to end. (12 sts.)
Next row: [P2tog] to end. (6 sts.)
Break yarn (leaving a long length for making up), thread through remaining 6 sts and draw up tightly.

TO MAKE UP

Sew center back seam, reversing the seam for the last few rows where it curls back. Make a Red pom-pom and attach to top of hat.

Below: *detail of Chilly Billy's hat and scarf*

Leo Lion

This happy little guy, with his fun bright spots and loopy mane is just waiting to be king of your home. The techniques used to create him are relatively easy to do and result in a lovely toy.

felted knitting

★
★
☆

SKILL LEVEL:
moderate

MEASUREMENTS
Approximately 13 in. (33 cm) tall

MATERIALS
- 2 x 25 g balls of Shetland Wool Brokers 2 ply Jumper Weight in Yellow 23
- 1 x 25 g ball of Shetland Wool Brokers 2 ply Jumper Weight in Gold 91
- 1 x 25 g ball of Shetland Wool Brokers 2 ply Jumper Weight in Purple 20
- 1 x 25 g ball of Shetland Wool Brokers 2 ply Jumper Weight in Orange 73
- 1 x 25 g ball of Shetland Wool Brokers 2 ply Jumper Weight in Royal 18
- 1 x 25 g ball of Shetland Wool Brokers 2 ply Jumper Weight in Red 93
- 1 x 25 g ball of Shetland Wool Brokers 2 ply Jumper Weight in Turquoise 132
- Pair of US 9 (5½ mm) knitting needles
- Stranded embroidery thread in Black and White
- Washable toy stuffing

ABBREVIATIONS
See page 10.

GAUGE
16 sts and 23 rows to 4 in. (10 cm) measured over stockinette stitch using US 9 (5½ mm) needles and 2 strands of yarn, before hand felting.

Note: Two strands of yarn are used together, throughout, for all pieces.

LION

BODY
Right leg

* With US 9 (5½ mm) needles and 2 strands of Gold, cast on 10 sts.
Next row: Inc 1 st, k wise, in every st. (20 sts.)
Beg with a p row, work 5 rows in st st.

Change to Yellow and cont as follows:
Beg with a k row, work 2 rows in st st. *
Row 9: K4 Yellow, k4 Purple, k12 Yellow.
Row 10: P11 Yellow, p6 Purple, p3 Yellow.
Row 11: K3 Yellow, k6 Purple, k11 Yellow.
Row 12: As Row 10.
Row 13: As Row 11.
Row 14: P12 Yellow, p4 Purple, p4 Yellow.
Row 15: K12 Yellow, k4 Orange, k4 Yellow.

Row 16: P3 Yellow, p6 Orange, p11 Yellow.

Row 17: K11 Yellow, k6 Orange, k3 Yellow.

Row 18: As Row 16.

Row 19: As Row 17.

Row 20: P4 Yellow, p4 Orange, p12 Yellow.

Place sts on a spare needle.

LEFT LEG

Work as for right leg from * to *.

Row 9: K4 Yellow, k4 Royal, k12 Yellow.

Row 10: P11 Yellow, p6 Royal, p3 Yellow.

Row 11: K3 Yellow, k6 Royal, k11 Yellow.

Row 12: As Row 10.

Row 13: As Row 11.

Row 14: P12 Yellow, p4 Royal, p4 Yellow.

Row 15: K12 Yellow, k4 Red, k4 Yellow.

Row 16: P3 Yellow, p6 Red, p11 Yellow.

Row 17: K11 Yellow, k6 Red, k3 Yellow.

Row 18: As Row 16.

Row 19: As Row 17.

Row 20: P4 Yellow, p4 Red, p12 Yellow.

Join legs

With RS facing:

Row 21: K4 Yellow, k4 Orange, k12 Yellow of left leg, then k2 Yellow, k4 Turquoise, k14 Yellow. (40 sts.)

Row 22: P13 Yellow, p6 Turquoise, p1 Yellow, m1, p11 Yellow, p6 Orange, p3 Yellow. (41 sts.)

Row 23: K3 Yellow, k6 Orange, k13 Yellow, k6 Turquoise, k13 Yellow.

Row 24: P13 Yellow, p6 Turquoise, p13 Yellow, p6 Orange, p3 Yellow.

Row 25: As Row 23.

Row 26: P14 Yellow, p4 Turquoise, p15 Yellow, p4 Orange, p4 Yellow.

Row 27: K13 Yellow, k4 Purple, k13 Yellow, k4 Royal, k7 Yellow.

Row 28: P6 Yellow, p6 Royal, p11 Yellow, p6 Purple, p12 Yellow.

Row 29: K12 Yellow, k6 Purple, k11 Yellow, k6 Royal, k6 Yellow.

Row 30: As Row 28.

Row 31: As Row 29.

Row 32: P7 Yellow, p4 Royal, p13 Yellow, p4 Purple, p13 Yellow.

Row 33: K5 Yellow, k4 Turquoise, k13 Yellow, k4 Red, k15 Yellow.

Row 34: P14 Yellow, p6 Red, p11 Yellow, p6 Turquoise, p4 Yellow.

Row 35: K4 Yellow, k6 Turquoise, k11 Yellow, k6 Red, k14 Yellow.

Row 36: As Row 34.

Row 37: As Row 35.

Row 38: P15 Yellow, p4 Red, p13 Yellow, p4 Turquoise, p5 Yellow.

Row 39: K14 Yellow, k4 Royal, k14 Yellow, k4 Orange, k5 Yellow.

Row 40: P4 Yellow, p6 Orange, p12 Yellow, p6 Royal, p13 Yellow.

Row 41: K13 Yellow, k6 Royal, k12 Yellow, k6 Orange, k4 Yellow.

Row 42: As Row 40.

Row 43: As Row 41.

Row 44: P5 Yellow, p4 Orange, p14 Yellow, p4 Royal, p14 Yellow.

Row 45: K6 Yellow, k4 Red, k14 Yellow, k4 Purple, k13 Yellow.

Row 46: P12 Yellow, p6 Purple, p12 Yellow, p6 Red, p5 Yellow.

Row 47: K5 Yellow, k6 Red, k12 Yellow, k6 Purple, k12 Yellow.

Row 48: As Row 46.

Row 49: As Row 47.

Row 50: P13 Yellow, p4 Purple, p14 Yellow, p4 Red, p6 Yellow.

Shape shoulders and neck

Cont in Yellow only as follows:

Next row: K9, skpo, k19, k2tog, k9. (39 sts.)

P 1 row.

Next row: K2, [k2tog, k1] to last 4 sts, k2tog, k2. (27 sts.)

P 1 row.

Next row: K2, [m1, k2] to last st, m1, k1. (40 sts.)

Beg with a p row, work 17 rows in st st.

Shape top of head

Next row: K3, [k2tog, k2] to last 5 sts, k2tog, k3. (31 sts.)

P 1 row.

Next row: K1, [k2tog] to end. (16 sts.)

Next row: [P2tog] to end. (8 sts.)

Bind off.

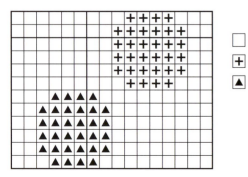

ARMS

Left arm

With US 9 (5½ mm) needles and 2 ends of Gold, cast on 8 sts.

Next row: Inc 1 st k wise in every st. (16 sts.)

Beg with a p row, work 5 rows in st st.

Working from Chart A, work 12 rows in st st.

Left: the tail is created by making a tube

Shape top

Cont in Yellow only as follows:

Beg with a k row, work 6 rows in st st, dec 1 st at each end of every row. (4 sts.)

Bind off.

Right arm

Work as for left arm, except work from Chart B.

EARS (Make 2)

With US 9 (5½ mm) needles and 2 ends of Yellow, cast on 4 sts.

Beg with a k row, work 2 rows in st st.

** **Next row:** Inc 1 st at each end of row. (6 sts.)

Beg with a p row, work 3 rows in st st.

Next row: Dec 1 st at each end of row. (4 sts.)

P 1 row. **

Rep from ** to ** once more.

Bind off.

MANE

With US 9 (5½ mm) needles and 2 ends of Gold, cast on 38 sts.

Next row: K1, [insert needle k wise into next st, place first two fingers of left hand at back of st, then wind yarn anti-clockwise round needle and fingers twice, draw through the 4 loops] to last st, k1.

Next row: K1, [k2tog, pulling loops down firmly] to last st, k1. (38 sts.)

Bind off.

TAIL

With US 9 (5½ mm) needles and 2 ends of Yellow, cast on 3 sts.

K 1 row, turn and sl all sts back onto the right needle.

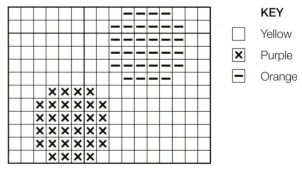

KEY

☐ Yellow
⊞ Turquoise
▲ Red

CHART A

KEY

☐ Yellow
☒ Purple
⊟ Orange

CHART B

Turn again, and pulling the yarn tight from the left side, k across the 3 sts. In this way you will k all rows and the row ends will pull together to make a tube.

Cont in this way until the tail measures 4 in. (10 cm). Bind off.

Cut 6 x 2¼ in. (6 cm) lengths of Gold and loop through one end of the tail using a crochet hook.

FELTING INSTRUCTIONS

Work in all ends with a needle.

Following the instructions on page 17 for hand felting, felt all pieces for approximately 30 minutes.

Reshape while damp, and dry thoroughly.

TO MAKE UP

Join inside leg seams, center back seam and center back head seam, leaving an opening halfway up the back. Stuff

Above: Leo Lion's bright and colorful mane

head firmly. Work a draw thread in yellow yarn and running stitch around neck decreases and increases, draw up tightly and fasten off.

Stuff legs and rest of body and close seam.

Join arm seams, leaving shaped edge open. Stuff and sew to sides of body at shoulders.

Sew ends of mane together to form a circle. Pin to head, stretching slightly, and stitch all around cast-off edge to secure. Stitch again under the knots.

Fold each ear in half and oversew row-ends and bottom edges together. Sew to head on top of mane.

Sew end of tail to center back, just above legs.

With black embroidery thread, work eyes and nose in satin stitch. Work stem stitch mouth in black. Sew a small white highlight in each eye.

Dylan Donkey

A soft, cuddly friend, with cute tufts of hair; Dylan Donkey is sure to become a firm favorite with your special little person.

felted knitting

★
★
☆

SKILL LEVEL:
moderate

MEASUREMENTS
Approximately 14 in. (35 cm) tall

MATERIALS
- 1 x 100 g ball of Rowan Scottish Tweed Chunky in Grey/Lewis Grey 7
- 1 x 100 g ball of Rowan Scottish Tweed Chunky in White/Porridge 24
- Pair of US 11 (8 mm) knitting needles
- Stranded embroidery thread in Black and White
- Washable toy stuffing

ABBREVIATIONS
See page 10.

GAUGE
11 sts and 15 rows to 4 in. (10 cm) measured over stockinette stitch using US 11 (8 mm) needles before machine felting.

DONKEY

BODY (Make 2)
With US 11 (8 mm) needles and Grey, cast on 14 sts.
Beg with a k row, work 4 rows in st st.
Next row: Inc 1 st at each end of row. (16 sts.)
Beg with a p row, work 9 rows in st st.
Beg with a k row, work 14 rows in st st, at the same time, dec 1 st at each end of every 3rd row. (8 sts.)
Bind off.

HEAD
With US 11 (8 mm) needles and Grey, cast on 12 sts.
Beg with a k row, work 2 rows in st st.
Next row: Inc 1 st k wise in every st. (24 sts.)
P 1 row.

Next row: K6, [m1, k2] 6 times, m1, k6. (31 sts.)
Beg with a p row, work 5 rows in st st.
Next row: K6, [k2tog, k1] 6 times, k2tog, k5. (24 sts.)
Beg with a p row, work 7 rows in st st.
Next row: [K2tog] to end. (12 sts.)
P 1 row.
Bind off.

MUZZLE
With US 11 (8 mm) needles and White, cast on 24 sts.
Beg with a k row, work 6 rows in st st.
Next row: K3, [k2tog, k2] to last 5 sts, k2tog, k3. (19 sts.)
P 1 row.
Next row: K1, [k2tog] to end. (10 sts.)
P 1 row.
Bind off.

Above: *side view of face*

EARS (Make 2 Grey, 2 White)

With US 11 (8 mm) needles and Grey, cast on 3 sts.
Beg with a k row, work 4 rows in st st.
Next row: K2tog, k1.
Next row: P2tog.
Break yarn, thread through rem st, pull tightly and fasten off.

LEGS (Make 2)

With US 11 (8 mm) needles and White, cast on 15 sts.
Beg with a k row, work 4 rows in st st.
Change to Grey and beg with a k row, work 12 rows in st st.
Bind off.

LEG BASES (Make 2)

With US 11 (8 mm) needles and White, cast on 4 sts.
Beg with a k row, work 2 rows in st st.
Next row: Inc 1 st at each end of row. (6 sts.)
P 1 row.
Next row: K2tog, k2, k2tog. (4 sts.)
P 1 row.
Bind off.

ARMS (Make 2)

With US 11 (8 mm) needles and White, cast on 12 sts.
Beg with a k row, work 4 rows in st st.

Change to Grey and beg with a k row, work 8 rows in st st.
Bind off 2 sts at beg of next 2 rows. (8 sts.)
Beg with a k row, work 3 rows in st st, at the same time dec 1 st at each end of every row. (2 sts.)
P 1 row.
Bind off.

ARM ENDS (Make 2)

With US 11 (8 mm) needles and White, cast on 2 sts.
Beg with a k row, work 2 rows in st st.
Next row: Inc 1 st in each st. (4 sts.)
P1 row.
Next row: [K2tog] twice. (2 sts.)
P 1 row.
Bind off.

FELTING INSTRUCTIONS

Work in all ends with a needle.
Hair: Before felting; take 10 x 3 in. (8 cm) lengths of Grey yarn and, following the fringing instructions, loop one length through each stitch of the cast-off edge of the head, ignoring the first and last stitch, and form a knot.
Following the instructions on page 17 for machine felting, felt all pieces in the washing machine on a 140°F (60°C) wash. Reshape while damp, and dry thoroughly.

TO MAKE UP

Join side seams of body.
Sew leg seams and then sew leg bases into each leg. Stuff firmly, then oversew the top edges, gathering slightly. Place the oversewn ends of the legs into the bottom opening of the body, and sew through all thicknesses. Stuff body firmly and close top opening.
Sew center back seam of head. Sew top of head together on right side, so that the tufts of hair are visible. Stuff head. Close seam at bottom of head.
Sew muzzle seam. Stuff and sew to front of head over shaping.
Sew one White and one Grey ear together for each ear. Then sew ears to head at either side of hair tufts.
Sew head to body.
Sew arm seams, then sew an end into each arm. Stuff firmly and sew to sides of body.
Embroider eyes and nostrils in satin stitch using black embroidery thread. Outline each eye with white embroidery thread. Sew a small white highlight in each eye.

Teddy

Children (and indeed most adults) can never have enough teddies. This little felted fellow is sure to be a great addition to any collection. Why not embroider an initial in the heart on his jumper for a truly individual touch?

felted knitting

SKILL LEVEL:
moderate

MEASUREMENTS
Approximately 12 in. (30 cm) tall

MATERIALS
- 1 x 100 g ball of UK Alpaca in Fawn
- Oddments of DK yarn in red and yellow
- Pair each of US 7 (4½ mm) and US 2/3 (3 mm) (use either US 2 or US 3, based on your gauge) knitting needles
- Stranded embroidery thread in Black and White
- Washable toy stuffing

ABBREVIATIONS
See page 10.

GAUGE
UK Alpaca DK
20 sts and 26 rows to 4 in. (10 cm) measured over stockinette stitch using US 7 (4½ mm) needles, before hand felting.
DK yarn
25 sts and 34 rows to 4 in. (10 cm) measured over stockinette stitch using US 2/3 (3 mm) needles.

TEDDY

BODY FRONT

With US 7 (4½ mm) needles and Fawn, cast on 5 sts.
K 1 row.
Beg with a p row, work 5 rows in st st, at the same time cast on 3 sts at beg of every row. (20 sts.)
Beg with a k row, work 34 rows in st st.
Bind off 4 sts at beg of next 2 rows. (12 sts.)
Bind off.

BODY BACK

*With US 7 (4½ mm) needles and Fawn, cast on 2 sts.
Beg with a k row, work 8 rows in st st, at the same time, inc 1 st at each end of Rows 2, 4 and 6. (8 sts.) *
Break yarn and place sts on a spare needle.
Make a second piece by rep from * to *.

Join pieces
With RS facing k across 8 sts of second piece, then 8 sts of first piece. (16 sts.)
Beg with a p row, work 3 rows in st st, inc 1 st at each end of Rows 1 and 3. (20 sts.)
Beg with a k row, work 36 rows in st st.
Bind off 4 sts at beg of next 2 rows. (12 sts.)
Bind off.

HEAD
Front

With US 7 (4½ mm) needles and Fawn, cast on 9 sts.
K 1 row.
Next row: P, inc 1 st at each end of row. (11 sts.)
Next row: K5, m1, k1, m1, k5. (13 sts.)
P 1 row.
Next row: K6, m1, k1, m1, k6. (15 sts.)
Next row: P, inc 1 st at each end of row. (17 sts.)
Next row: K8, m1, k1, m1, k8. (19 sts.)

Above: leg detail

P 1 row.

Next row: K9, m1, k1, m1, k9. (21 sts.)

Next row: P, inc 1 st at each end of row. (23 sts.)

Next row: K11, m1, k1, m1, k11. (25 sts.)

Beg with a p row, work 3 rows in st st.

Next row: K12, cast off 1 st, k11.

Work on these 12 sts only as follows:

** **Next row:** P to last 2 sts, p2tog.

Next row: Skpo, k to end.

Rep the last 2 rows twice. (6 sts.)

Now, beg with a p row, work 7 rows in st st, dec 1 st at each end of Rows 3 and 6. (2 sts.)

Bind off. **

With WS facing, rejoin yarn to rem 12 sts and work from ** to **, reversing all shapings.

GUSSET

With US 7 (4½ mm) needles and Fawn, cast on 7 sts.

Beg with a k row, work 16 rows in st st. inc 1 st at each end of every 4th row. (15 sts.)

Beg with a k row, work 10 rows in st st.

Beg with a k row, work 21 rows in st st, dec 1 st at each end of every 3rd row. (1 st.)

Break yarn and pull through rem st.

ARMS (Make 2)

With US 7 (4½ mm) needles and Fawn, cast on 17 sts.

Beg with a k row, work 28 rows in st st.

Next row: K1, [k2tog, k1] to last st, k1. (12 sts.)

P 1 row.

Next row: [K2tog] to end. (6 sts.)

Break yarn, thread through rem sts, and draw up tightly.

LEGS (Make 2)

With US 7 (4½ mm) needles and Fawn, cast on 13 sts.

Shape foot

Row 1: K1, m1, k5, m1, k1, m1, k5, m1, k1. (17 sts.)

P 1 row.

Next row: K1, m1, k5, [m1, k1] 6 times, k4, m1, k1. (25 sts.)

Next row: P11, [m1, p1] 4 times, p10. (29 sts.)

Beg with a k row, work 2 rows in st st.

Next row: K11, [k2tog] 4 times, k10. (25 sts.)

P 1 row.

Next row: K9, [k2tog] 4 times, k8. (21 sts.)

Beg with a p row, work 31 rows in st st.

Bind off.

EARS (Make 2)

With US 7 (4½ mm) needles and Fawn, cast on 6 sts.

Work in seed st throughout, as follows:

Row 1: [K1, p1] to end.

Row 2: [P1, k1] to end.

Incorporating the new sts in to the pattern, inc 1 st at each end of the next row. (8 sts.)

Work 5 rows in seed st.

Dec 1 st at each end of foll 2 rows. (4 sts.)

Bind off.

FELTING INSTRUCTIONS

Work in all ends with a needle.

Following the instructions on page 17 for hand felting, felt all pieces for approximately 20 minutes.

Reshape while damp, and dry thoroughly.

TO MAKE UP

Sew seam at bottom of back body piece. Sew sole, heel and center back seam of each leg. Stuff, then oversew top edges together. Lay tops of legs along slopes at bottom of front body piece and then lay back body piece on top. Sew together through all thicknesses. Sew arm seams, leaving top open. Stuff and oversew top edges together. Sew side seams of body to 1½ in. (4 cm) from top. Sew arms into side seams of body and sew shoulder seams. Stuff body and close seam. Starting at the bottom edge, sew gusset to front head. Stuff firmly, molding as you go. Sew ears to top of head, placing edge of ear to gusset seam. Sew head to body. Embroider eyes and nose in satin stitch, and mouth in stem stitch, using black. Sew a small white highlight in each eye.

CLOTHES

JUMPER

Front

* With US 2/3 (3 mm) needles and Yellow, cast on
28 sts.

Beg with a k row, work 2 rows in st st.

Next row: [K2, p2] to end.

Rep the last row once more. *

Change to Red, and beg with a k row, work 6 rows in st st.

Place motif

Next row: K9, k across 9 sts of Row 1 of chart, k10.

Cont working rem 9 rows of chart in st st.

Beg with a k row, work 6 rows in st st.

Shape neck

** **Next row:** K10, cast off 8 sts, k10.

Cont on these 10 sts only as follows:

Next row: P to last 2 sts, p2tog. (9 sts.)

Next row: Bind off 2 sts, k to end. (7 sts.)

P 1 row.

Bind off.

With WS facing, rejoin yarn to rem 10 sts and cont as follows:

Next row: Bind off 2 sts, p to end. (8 sts.)

Next row: K to last 2 sts, k2tog. (7 sts.)

P 1 row.

Bind off. **

Below: *detail of jumper*

BACK

Work as for front from * to *

Change to Red, and beg with a k row, work 22 rows in st st.

Shape neck

Work as for front from ** to **.

SLEEVES (Make 2)

With US 2/3 (3 mm) needles and Yellow, cast on
24 sts.

Beg with a k row, work 2 rows in st st.

Next row: [K2, p2] to end.

Rep the last row once more.

Change to Red, and beg with a k row, work 10 rows in st st.
Bind off.

NECK TRIM

Join right shoulder seam.

With RS facing and US 2/3 (3 mm) needles and Yellow, pick up and k 3 sts down side front neck, 8 sts across center front neck, 3 sts up side front neck, 3 sts down side back neck, 8 sts across center back neck, and
3 sts up side back neck. (28 sts.)

Next row: [K2, p2] to end.

Rep the last row once more.

Beg with a p row, work 2 rows in st st.

Bind off.

TO MAKE UP

Join left shoulder seam. Lay the front and back pieces flat and sew sleeves to sides making sure to center them at the shoulder seams. Sew both under arm and side seams.

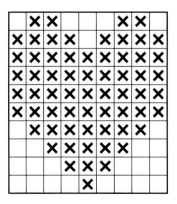

KEY

☐	Red
☒	Yellow

CHART

Ballerina

All set for her star performance, this pretty ballerina is sure to be a hit with any little girl. Her tutu and ballet shoes are removable for hours of make-believe fun.

MEASUREMENTS
Approximately 12 in. (30 cm) tall

MATERIALS
- 1 x 100 g ball of King Cole Big Value Baby DK in Lilac 17
- 1 x 100 g ball of King Cole Big Value Baby DK in Peach 59
- 1 x 50 g ball of King Cole Sprinkles in Lychee 634
- Small amount of King Cole Big Value DK in Elderberry 140
- Pair each of US 2/3 (3 mm) (use either US 2 or US 3, based on your gauge) and US 5 (3¾ mm) knitting needles

- Stranded embroidery thread in Black, White, Flesh tone and Pink
- Washable toy stuffing
- ¼ in. (7 mm) and ⅛ in. (3 mm) wide Lilac ribbon
- 2 x Lilac ribbon roses
- 1 x press stud fastener

ABBREVIATIONS
See page 10.

GAUGE
Big Value Baby DK
25 sts and 34 rows to 4 in. (10 cm) measured over stockinette stitch using US 2/3 (3 mm) needles.

DOLL

BODY & HEAD
With US 2/3 (3 mm) needles and Lilac, cast on 53 sts.
Place markers at the 16th and 38th st.
Beg with a k row, work 32 rows in st st.
Next row (RS): P.
Next row: K.
Change to Peach and beg with a k row work 2 rows in st st.
Shape shoulders
Next row: K13, k2tog, k23, k2tog, k13. (51 sts.)
P 1 row.
Next row: K13, k2tog, k21, k2tog, k13. (49 sts.)
P 1 row.

Next row: K12, k2tog, k21, k2tog, k12. (47 sts.)
P 1 row.
Next row: K1, [k2tog] to last 2 sts, k2. (25 sts.)
P 1 row.
K 1 row, placing markers at each end of this row.
P 1 row
Shape head
Next row: K1, [k1, m1] to last st, k1. (48 sts.)
P 1 row.
Next row: K13, m1, k22, m1, k13. (50 sts.)
P 1 row.
Next row: K13, m1, k1, m1, k22, m1, k1, m1, k13. (54 sts.)
Beg with a p row, work 21 rows in st st.

Shape top of head

Next row: [K2, k2tog] to last 2 sts, k2. (41 sts.)

P 1 row.

Next row: K1, [k2tog] to last 2 sts, k2. (22 sts.)

P 1 row.

Next row: [K2tog] to end. (11 sts.)

Next row: [P2tog] to last st, p1. (6 sts.)

Break yarn (leaving a long length for making up), thread through rem 6 sts and draw up tightly.

BODY BASE

With US 2/3 (3 mm) needles and Lilac, cast on 10 sts.

Beg with a k row, work 2 rows in st st.

Next row: Cast on 2 sts, k to end.

Next row: Cast on 2 sts, p to end.

Rep the last 2 rows once more. (18 sts.)

Next row: Inc 1, k to last st, inc 1.

P 1 row.

Rep the last 2 rows once more. (22 sts.)

Work 2 rows in st st.

Next row: Skpo, k18, k2tog. (20 sts.)

P 1 row.

Next row: Skpo, k16, k2tog. (18 sts.)

Next row: Bind off 2 sts, p to end.

Next row: Bind off 2 sts, k to end.

Rep the last 2 rows once more. (10 sts.)

P 1 row.

Bind off.

LEGS (Make 2)

With US 2/3 (3 mm) needles and Peach, cast on 26 sts.

Beg with a k row, work 32 rows in st st.

Shape instep

Next row: K16, turn.

Next row: P6, turn.

Working on these 6 sts only, work 8 rows in st st.

Break yarn and leave these sts on a spare needle.

With RS facing, rejoin yarn at base of instep and k up 7 sts down side of instep, k 6 sts from spare needle, k up 7 sts up other side of instep and k rem 10 sts. (40 sts.)

Beg with a p row, work 3 rows in st st.

Shape sole

Next row: K1, skpo, k13, skpo, k4, k2tog, k13, k2tog, k1. (36 sts.)

P 1 row.

Next row: K1, skpo, k12, skpo, k2, k2tog, k12, k2tog, k1. (32 sts.)

P 1 row.

Next row: K1, [k2tog] to last st, k1. (17 sts.)

P 1 row.

Bind off.

ARMS (Make 2)

With US 2/3 (3 mm) needles and Peach, cast on 6 sts.

Beg with a k row, work 2 rows in st st.

Next row: K1, m1, k to last st, m1, k1.

P 1 row.

Rep the last 2 rows until there are 18 sts.

Beg with a k row, work 18 rows in st st.

Shape hand

Next row: K9, m1, k9. (19 sts.)

P 1 row.

Next row: K9, m1, k1, m1, k9. (21 sts.)

P 1 row.

Next row: K9, m1, k3, m1, k9. (23 sts.)

P 1 row.

Next row: K9, m1, k5, m1, k9. (25 sts.)

P 1 row.

Next row: K9, [skpo] twice, [k2tog] twice, k8. (21 sts.)

Next row: P8, [p2tog] twice, p9. (19 sts.)

Next row: K9, k2tog, k8. (18 sts.)

P 1 row.

Next row: K1, skpo, k4, [k2tog] twice, k4, k2tog, k1. (14 sts.)

P 1 row.

Next row: K1, [k2tog] to last st, k1. (8 sts.)

Next row: [K2tog] 4 times.

Break yarn, thread through rem 4 sts and draw up tightly.

TO MAKE UP

Join sole, heel and center back seam of each leg and stuff firmly. Oversew cast-on edges together.

Using the yarn length left from drawing up sts on top of head, join center back seam of head and body, leaving the bottom 1½ in. (4 cm) open.

Place the tops of the legs between the markers at front of body, laying the legs inside the body piece, pin the body base to lower edge of body and backstitch through all thicknesses. Turn to right side through opening. Stuff head firmly. Wind a length of Peach yarn tightly around the neck at markers and secure. Stuff body and close seam.

Above: the ballerina's hair is tied with a pretty lilac ribbon

Join underarm seams and stuff firmly. Attach tops of arms to sides of body over shoulder shaping.

Cut lengths of Elderberry yarn approx 25½ in. (65 cm) long. Backstitch lengths into position, just to side of center to form a side parting, from front to just beyond top of head. Smooth all strands and gather at nape of neck, stitching to back of neck. Divide strands into 3 equal groups and plait to end. Tie a length of ¼ in. (7 mm) wide ribbon around end and make a bow. Attach a ribbon rose to a length of ¼ in. (7 mm) wide ribbon, wrap around head securing at back under base of plait.

With black embroidery thread, work eyes in satin stitch. Sew a small white highlight in the top corner of each eye. Work straight stitch eyelashes above each eye. Using stem stitch, work nose in flesh tone thread and mouth in pink thread.

CLOTHES

LEOTARD STRAPS (Make 2)

With US 2/3 (3 mm) needles and Lilac, cast on 19 sts. Bind off.

Place leotard straps over each shoulder and catch to top of reverse st st at front and back. Sew a ribbon rose to center front of leotard.

SHOES (Make 2)

With US 2/3 (3 mm) needles and Lilac, cast on 30 sts.
K 1 row.
Next row: P15, m1, p15. (31 sts.)
Next row: K15, m1, k1, m1, k15. (33 sts.)
P 1 row.
Next row: K15, m1, k3, m1, k15. (35 sts.)
P 1 row.
Next row: K15, m1, k5, m1, k15. (37 sts.)
P 1 row.
Next row: K1, skpo, k12, skpo, k3, k2tog, k12, k2tog, k1. (33 sts.)
P 1 row.
Next row: K1, [k2tog] to last 2 sts, k2. (18 sts.)
Next row: P1, p2tog, p4, [p2tog] twice, p4, p2tog, p1. (14 sts.)
Bind off.

Join heel and sole seam. Cut four 12 in. (30 cm) lengths of ⅛ in. (3 mm) wide ribbon, and sew inside sides of shoes. Wrap around legs and tie in bows at the back.

TUTU

With US 5 (3¾ mm) needles and Lychee, cast on 186 sts.
K 2 rows.
Change to US 2/3 (3 mm) needles and Lilac.
Beg with a k row, work 14 rows in st st.
Next row: K1, [k2tog] to last st, k1. (94 sts.)
Next row: P1, [p2tog] to last st, p1. (48 sts.)
Next row: Cast on 5 sts, p 1 row. (53 sts.)
Next row: Cast on 5 sts, k 1 row. (58 sts.)
K 2 rows.
Bind off.

Join center back seam of Tutu, leaving the top 1¼ in. (3 cm) open. Sew press stud to waistband where it overlaps.

Baby

This sweet little baby in its soft sleepsuit would make a lovely gift for a new arrival or a loving toddler. As it only uses small amounts of yarn, why not knit a whole nursery full?

plain
knitting

★
★
☆

SKILL LEVEL:
moderate

MEASUREMENTS
Approximately 10 in. (26 cm) tall

MATERIALS
- 1 x 25 g ball of Wendy Courtelle DK in Flesh Beige 959
- 1 x 50 g ball of Peter Pan Darling in Lemon 362
- Small amount of Peter Pan Darling in Raffia 366
- Pair of US 3 (3¼ mm) knitting needles
- Stranded embroidery thread in Black, White, Flesh tone and Pink
- Washable toy stuffing

ABBREVIATIONS
See page 10.

GAUGE
Peter Pan Darling
20 sts and 30 rows to 4 in. (10 cm) measured over stockinette stitch using US 3 (3¼ mm) needles.
Wendy Courtelle DK
23 sts and 34 rows to 4 in. (10 cm) measured over stockinette stitch using US 3 (3¼ mm) needles.

BABY

BODY & HEAD
With US 3 (3¼ mm) needles and Lemon, cast on 32 sts.
Beg with a k row, work 22 rows in st st.
Head
Change to Flesh Beige and beg with a k row work 8 rows in st st.
Hair
Using the intarsia method cont as follows:
Next row: P8 Raffia, k16 Flesh Beige, p8 Raffia.
Next row: K8, p2 Raffia, p12 Flesh Beige, p2 Raffia, k8 Raffia.

Next row: P10, k1 Raffia, k10 Flesh Beige, k1 Raffia, p10 Raffia.
Next row: K11, p1 Raffia, p8 Flesh Beige, p1 Raffia, k11 Raffia.
Next row: P12 Raffia, k8 Flesh Beige, p12 Raffia.
Next row: K12, p1 Raffia, p6 Flesh Beige, p1 Raffia, k12 Raffia.
Next row: All sts in Raffia, p13, k6, p13.
K 1 row.
Next row: P7, p2tog, p14, p2tog, p7. (30 sts.)
K 1 row.
Next row: P6, [p2tog] twice, p10, [p2tog] twice, p6. (26 sts.)
Beg with a k row, work 4 rows in rev st st.
Next row: K1, [k1, k2tog] to last st, k1. (18 sts.)
Next row: P1, [p2tog] to last st, p1. (10 sts.)
Break yarn, thread through rem sts and draw up tightly.

BODY BASE

With US 3 (3¼ mm) needles and Lemon, cast on 6 sts.

Beg with a k row, work 2 rows in st st.

Inc 1 st at each end of the next 4 rows (14 sts.)

Work 4 rows.

Dec 1 st at each end of the next 4 rows. (6 sts.)

Work 2 rows.

Bind off.

LEGS (Make 2)

With US 3 (3¼ mm) needles and Lemon, cast on 14 sts.

Beg with a k row, work 8 rows in st st.

Shape knee

Next row: K11, turn.

Next row: P8, turn.

Next row: K9, turn.

Next row: P10, turn.

Next row: K11, turn.

Next row: P12, turn.

Next row: K13, turn.

P 1 row.

Beg with a k row, work 8 rows in st st.

Next row: K1, m1, k4, [k1, m1] 3 times, k5, m1, k1. (19 sts.)

Work 3 rows in st st.

Next row: K1, k2tog, k5, [k2tog] twice, k4, k2tog, k1. (15 sts.)

P 1 row.

Bind off.

ARMS (Make 2)

With US 3 (3¼ mm) needles and Lemon, cast on 10 sts.

Beg with a k row, work 6 rows in st st.

Shape elbow

Next row: K8, turn.

Next row: P6, turn.

Next row: K7, turn.

Next row: P8, turn.

Next row: K9, turn.

P 1 row.

Beg with a k row, work 6 rows in st st.

Change to Flesh Beige and work 6 rows in st st.

Next row: K1, [k2tog] to last st, k1. (6 sts.)

Break yarn, thread through rem sts and draw up tightly.

TO MAKE UP

Join center back seam of body and head.

Join foot and center back seam of each leg. Stuff firmly and oversew top edges together. Pin top of legs to front bottom edge of body. Pin body base over leg tops and stitch through all thicknesses, leaving an opening.

Stuff head firmly. Run a draw thread of yarn around neck where yarn changes, draw up tightly and fasten off.

Stuff remainder of body and close opening.

Sew underarm seams and stuff firmly. Sew to sides of body. Embroider eyes in satin stitch using black embroidery thread. Sew eyelashes in black, using small straight stitches. Sew a small white highlight in each eye. Embroider nose in stem stitch using flesh tone embroidery thread. Embroider mouth in stem stitch and satin stitch using pink embroidery thread.

Left: *detail of face and hair*

Mermaid

A lovely soft cotton yarn combines with a beautiful fancy effect to create this Mermaid. Her flowing auburn hair and shell bikini top complete the picture.

plain
knitting

SKILL LEVEL:
moderate

MEASUREMENTS
Approximately 13 in. (33 cm) tall

MATERIALS
- 1 x 50 g ball of Sirdar Luxury Soft Cotton in Pink/Flamingo 651
- 1 x 50 g ball of Sirdar Medici in Laguna 160
- Small amounts of Sirdar Luxury Soft Cotton in Blue 664 and Lilac 659
- Small amount of Sirdar Snuggly DK in Orange 357
- Pair of US 3 (3¼ mm) knitting needles

- Stranded embroidery thread in Black, White, Flesh tone and Pink
- Washable toy stuffing

ABBREVIATIONS
See page 10.

GAUGE
Luxury Soft Cotton
24 sts and 33 rows to 4 in. (10 cm) measured over stockinette stitch, using US 3 (3¼ mm) needles.
Medici
23 sts and 42 rows to 4 in. (10 cm) measured over garter stitch using US 3 (3¼ mm) needles.

MERMAID

BODY & HEAD
With US 3 (3¼ mm) needles and Pink, cast on 50 sts.
Beg with a k row, work 12 rows in st st.
Change to Blue.
Next row: K.
Next row (WS): K.
Next row (RS): P.
Beg with a p row work 5 rows in st st.
Next row (RS): P.
Next row: K.
Change to Pink.
Shape shoulders
Next row: K12, skpo, k22, k2tog, k12. (48 sts.)

P 1 row.
Next row: K11, skpo, k22, k2tog, k11. (46 sts.)
P 1 row.
Next row: K11, skpo, k20, k2tog, k11. (44 sts.)
P 1 row.
Next row: K1, [k2tog] to last st, k1. (23 sts.)
P 1 row.
K 1 row, placing markers at each end of this row.
P 1 row.
Shape head
Next row: K1, [m1, k1] to end. (45 sts.)
P 1 row.
Next row: K8, [m1, k7] 4 times, m1, k9. (50 sts.)
Beg with a p row, work 21 rows in st st.
Shape top of head
Next row: [K2, k2tog] to last 2 sts, k2. (38 sts.)

P 1 row.

Next row: K1, [k2tog] to last st, k1. (20 sts.)

P 1 row.

Next row: [K2tog] to end. (10 sts.)

Next row: P1, [p2tog] to last st, p1.

Break yarn (leaving a long length for making up), thread through rem 6 sts and draw up tightly.

FISH TAIL (Make 2)

Worked in g st throughout.

First fin

* With US 3 (3¼ mm) needles and Laguna, cast on 5 sts.

K 1 row.

Inc 1 st at each end of next 2 rows. (9 sts.)

Then inc 1 st at each end of foll 2 alt rows. (13 sts.) *

Break yarn and place sts on a spare needle.

Second fin

Work as for first fin from * to *.

Join fins

With RS facing, k across 13 sts of second fin, then 13 sts of first fin. (26 sts.)

K 6 rows.

Bind off 7 sts at beg of next 2 rows. (12 sts.)

Then dec 1 st at each end of next and foll alt row. (8 sts.)

K 6 rows.

Inc 1 st at each end of next and 2 foll 4th rows. (14 sts.)

Then inc 1 st at each end of every foll 3rd row to 26 sts.

K 12 rows.

Bind off.

ARMS (Make 2)

With US 3 (3¼ mm) needles and Pink, cast on 6 sts.

Beg with a k row, work 2 rows in st st.

Next row: K1, m1, k to last st, m1, k1. (8 sts.)

P 1 row.

Rep the last 2 rows until there are 18 sts.

Beg with a k row, work 12 rows in st st.

Shape hand

Next row: K9, m1, k9. (19 sts.)

P 1 row.

Next row: K9, m1, k1, m1, k9. (21 sts.)

P 1 row.

Next row: K9, m1, k3, m1, k9. (23 sts.)

P 1 row.

Next row: K9, skpo, k1, k2tog, k9. (21 sts.)

Next row: P8, [p2tog] twice, p9. (19 sts.)

Next row: K1, skpo, k4, [k2tog] twice, k4, k2tog, k2. (15 sts.)

P 1 row.

Next row: K1, [k2tog] to end. (8 sts.)

Next row: [P2tog] 4 times.

Break yarn, thread through rem 4 sts and draw up tightly.

TO MAKE UP

Sew the fish tail pieces together at sides and bottom, leaving the top open.

Sew center back seam of body and head, leaving the last 1½ in. (4 cm) open for stuffing. Sew body to tail.

Stuff head firmly. Then run a draw thread of Pink yarn around neck at markers, pull tightly and fasten off. Stuff remainder of body and tail. Close opening.

Sew underarm seams of each arm. Stuff and sew to sides of body over shoulder shaping.

Left: *detail of tail showing the fancy-effect yarn used*

CLOTHES

SHELL TOP STRAPS (Make 2)
With US 3 (3¼ mm) needles and Blue, cast on 15 sts.
Bind off.

SHELLS (Make 2)
With US 3 (3¼ mm) needles and Lilac, cast on 3 sts.
K 2 rows.
Next row: [K1, m1] twice, k1. (5 sts.)
Next row: [P1, k1] twice, p1.
Next row: [K1, m1, p1, m1] twice, k1. (9 sts.)
Next row: [P1, k1] to last st, p1.
Next row: K1, m1, [p1, k1] 3 times, p1, m1, k1. (11 sts.)
Next row: P1, k2, [p1, k1] twice, p1, k2, p1.
Next row: K1, p2, k1, m1, p1, k1, m1, p1, k1, p2, k1. (13 sts.)
Next row: Bind off 4 sts, k1, [p1, k2] twice, p1.
Next row: Bind off 4 sts, p1, k1, p2.
Bind off rem 5 sts in patt as set.

TO MAKE UP
Sew straps over shoulders catching to top of reverse stockinette stitch at front and back.
Sew shells to front of top.
Hair: Cut 16 in. (40 cm) lengths of Orange yarn and lay on head. Sew to head in a line from front to back of head to form a center parting. Carefully separate the yarn with a pin or needle to form soft curls. Smooth down hair and divide into two bunches. Thread small lengths of Lilac yarn through the knitted fabric at each side of head and tie around bunches. Knot and secure. Trim hair to an equal length. Embroider eyes in satin stitch using black embroidery thread. Sew eyelashes in black, using small straight stitches. Sew a small white highlight in each eye. Embroider nose in stem stitch using flesh tone embroidery thread. Embroider mouth and tummy button in stem stitch using pink embroidery thread.

Below: *detail showing face, hair and bikini top*

Mommy Bunny

This gorgeous bunny and her babies would make a delightful addition to any nursery. The baby bunnies are finger puppets and will provide hours of nursery rhyme fun.

felted knitting

★
★
☆

**SKILL LEVEL:
moderate**

MEASUREMENTS
Approximately 14 in. (36 cm) tall

MATERIALS
- 3 x 25 g balls of Shetland Wool Brokers 2 ply Jumper Weight in Primrose 96
- 2 x 25 g balls of Shetland Wool Brokers 2 ply Jumper Weight in Cream 1A
- 2 x 25 g balls of Shetland Wool Brokers 2 ply Jumper Weight in Pink 101
- 1 x 25 g ball of Shetland Wool Brokers 2 ply Jumper Weight in Pale Blue 14
- Pair of US 9 (5½ mm) knitting needles
- Stranded embroidery thread in Black and White
- Washable toy stuffing

ABBREVIATIONS
See page 10.

GAUGE
16 sts and 23 rows to 4 in. (10 cm) measured over stockinette stitch using US 9 (5½ mm) needles and 2 strands of yarn, before machine felting.

Note: Two strands of yarn are used together, throughout, for all pieces.

MUMMY BUNNY

BODY
With US 9 (5½ mm) needles and 2 strands of Primrose, cast on 24 sts.
Beg with a k row, work 2 rows in st st.
Next row: K1, [m1, k2] to last st, m1, k1. (36 sts.)
Beg with a p row, work 31 rows in st st.
Next row: K1, [k2tog, k2] to last 3 sts, k2tog, k1. (27 sts.)
P 1 row.
Bind off.

HEAD
Front Section
With US 9 (5½ mm) needles and 2 strands of Primrose, cast on 23 sts.
Beg with a k row, work 2 rows in st st.
Next row: K11, m1, k1, m1, k11. (25 sts.)
Beg with a p row, work 3 rows in st st.
Next row: K12, m1, k1, m1, k12. (27 sts.)
Beg with a p row, work 3 rows in st st.
Next row: K13, m1, k1, m1, k13. (29 sts.)
P 1 row.
Bind off.

Gusset
With US 9 (5½ mm) needles and 2 strands of Primrose, cast on 3 sts.

Above: *embroider the features with care*

Beg with a k row, work 2 rows in st st.

Then, beg with a k row, work 10 rows in st st, inc 1 st at each end of every k row. (13 sts.)

Now, beg with a k row, work 16 rows in st st.

Then, beg with a k row, work 10 rows in st st, dec 1 st at each end of every k row. (3 sts.)

Beg with a k row, work 2 rows in st st.

Bind off.

EARS (Make 2 Primrose, 2 Pink)

With US 9 (5½ mm) needles and 2 strands of Primrose, cast on 6 sts.

Beg with a k row, work 16 rows in st st.

Next row: Skpo, k2, k2tog. (4 sts.)

Next row: [P2tog] twice. (2 sts.)

Bind off.

ARMS (Make 2)

With US 9 (5½ mm) needles and 2 strands of Primrose, cast on 14 sts.

Beg with a k row, work 26 rows in st st.

Next row: [K2tog] to end. (7 sts.)

P 1 row.

Bind off.

LEGS (Make 2)

With US 9 (5½ mm) needles and 2 strands of Primrose, cast on 17 sts.

P 1 row.

Shape foot

Next row: K1, m1, k5, [m1, k1] 5 times, k5, m1, k1. (24 sts.)

P 1 row.

Next row: K1, m1, k10, m1, k2, m1, k10, m1, k1. (28 sts.)

Beg with a p row, work 5 rows in st st.

Next row: K1, skpo, k9, skpo, k2tog, k9, k2tog, k1. (24 sts.)

P 1 row.

Next row: K1, skpo, k5, [skpo] twice, [k2tog] twice, k5, k2tog, k1. (18 sts.)

Next row: P6, cast off 6 sts, p5.

Next row: K across all 12 sts.

Beg with a p row, work 27 rows in st st.

Bind off.

FELTING INSTRUCTIONS

Work in all ends with a needle.

Following the instructions on page 17 for machine felting, felt all pieces in the washing machine on a 140°F (60°C) wash. Reshape while damp, and dry thoroughly.

TO MAKE UP

Sew center back seam of body.

Sew top of foot, sole seam and center back seam of each leg. Stuff and oversew top edges.

Place legs inside bottom edge of body and sew seam at bottom through all thicknesses. Stuff body and close top seam.

Sew head pieces together, leaving an opening. Stuff firmly and close opening.

Sew head to body.

Sew arm seams and stuff. Sew to sides of body.

Sew one Primrose and one Pink ear together for each ear. Sew ears to head.

Embroider eyes and nose in satin stitch, using black embroidery thread. Embroider mouth in stem stitch using black embroidery thread. Sew a small white highlight in each eye.

DRESS

PINAFORE

With US 9 (5½ mm) needles and 2 strands of Pale Blue, cast on 80 sts.

K 2 rows.

Change to Pink, and beg with a k row, work 38 rows in st st.

Next row: [K2tog] to end. (40 sts.)

Beg with a p row, work 7 rows in st st.

Change to Pale Blue and k 3 rows.

Bind off.

POCKET

With US 9 (5½ mm) needles and 2 strands of Pink, cast on 40 sts.

Beg with a k row, work 8 rows in st st.

Change to Pale Blue and k 3 rows.

Bind off.

STRAPS (Make 2)

With US 9 (5½ mm) needles and 2 strands of Pale Blue, cast on 12 sts.

K 1 row.

Bind off.

FELTING INSTRUCTIONS

Work in all ends with a needle.

Following the instructions on page 17 for machine felting, felt all pieces in the washing machine on a 140°F (60°C) wash. Reshape while damp, and dry thoroughly.

TO MAKE UP

Sew center back seam.

Sew pocket to lower edge. Then sew through all thicknesses to divide pocket into five separate pockets. Place pinafore on rabbit and sew straps to top edges over shoulders.

BABY BUNNIES

BABY BUNNIES (Make 5)

With US 9 (5½ mm) needles and 2 strands of Cream, cast on 14 sts.

K 2 rows.

Beg with a k row, work 14 rows in st st.

Next row: K1, [k2tog] to last st, k1. (8 sts.)

Next row: [P2tog] to end. (4 sts.)

Break yarn, thread through rem sts, pull tightly and fasten off.

EARS (Make 10)

With US 9 (5½ mm) needles and 2 strands of Cream, cast on 3 sts.

Beg with a k row, work 4 rows in st st.

Next row: K2tog, k1. (2 sts.)

Next row: P2tog. (1 st.)

Break yarn, thread through rem st, pull tightly and fasten off.

FELTING INSTRUCTIONS

Work in all ends with a needle.

Following the instructions on page 17 for machine felting, felt all pieces in the washing machine on a 140°F (60°C) wash. Reshape while damp, and dry thoroughly.

TO MAKE UP

Sew center back seam of each bunny. With p side to front, sew ears to top.

Embroider eyes and nose in satin stitch, using black embroidery thread. Embroider mouth in stem stitch using black embroidery thread.

Left: the baby bunnies fit neatly into mommy's apron

Magic Unicorn

Unicorns are the stuff of fairytales; just the thing for your little princes and princesses to have endless fun with.

plain knitting

★
★
☆

SKILL LEVEL: **moderate**

MEASUREMENTS

Approximately 11 in. (28 cm) long

MATERIALS

- 2 x 50 g balls of Sirdar Snuggly Pearls DK in Lilac 219
- 1 x 50 g ball of Sirdar Snuggly Pearls DK in White 251
- Small amount of Sirdar Denim Ultra in 640
- Pair of US 2/3 (3 mm) (use either US 2 or US 3, based on your gauge) knitting needles

- Stranded embroidery thread in Black and White
- Washable toy stuffing

ABBREVIATIONS

See page 10.

GAUGE

26 sts and 38 rows to 4 in. (10 cm) measured over stockinette stitch using US 2/3 (3 mm) needles.

UNICORN

BODY

With US 2/3 (3 mm) needles and Lilac, cast on 16 sts.

Beg with a k row, work 2 rows in st st.

Next row: [K1, m1] to last st, k1.

P 1 row.

Rep the last 2 rows once more. (61 sts.)

Next row: [K15, m1] 3 times, k16. (64 sts.)

Beg with a p row, work 71 rows in st st.

Next row: K15, [k2tog, k14] twice, k2tog, k15. (61 sts.)

P 1 row.

Next row: K1, [k2tog] to end.

P 1 row.

Rep the last 2 rows once more. (16 sts.)

Bind off.

LEGS (Make 4)

With US 2/3 (3 mm) needles and White, cast on 32 sts.

Beg with a k row, work 8 rows in st st.

Change to Lilac, and beg with a k row, work 16 rows in st st.

Beg with a k row, work 6 rows in st st, inc 1 st at each end of the next and foll 2 alt rows. (38 sts.)

Shape top

Bind off 5 sts at beg of next 2 rows. (28 sts.)

Bind off 3 sts at beg of next 2 rows. (22 sts.)

Beg with a k row, work 8 rows in st st, dec 1 st at each end of the next and foll alt rows. (14 sts.)

Bind off 3 sts at beg of next 4 rows. (2 sts.)

Bind off.

LEG BASES (Make 4)

With US 2/3 (3 mm) needles and White, cast on 2 sts.

K 1 row.

Inc 1 st at each end of next 4 rows. (10 sts.)

Beg with a p row, work 5 rows in st st.

Dec 1 st at each end of next 4 rows. (2 sts.)

Bind off.

HEAD

With US 2/3 (3 mm) needles and Lilac, cast on 58 sts.

Beg with a k row, work 12 rows in st st.

Next row: K4, [k2tog, k5] 7 times, K2tog, k3. (50 sts.)

P 1 row.

Next row: K16, [m1, k2] 9 times, m1, k16. (60 sts.)

P 1 row.

Next row: K54, turn.

Next row: P48, turn.

Next row: K42, turn.

Next row: P36, turn.

Next row: K35, turn.

Next row: P34, turn.

Next row: K33, turn.

Next row: P32, turn.

Next row: K31, turn.

Next row: P30, turn.

Next row: K29, turn.

Next row: P28, turn.

Next row: K27, turn.

Next row: P26, turn.

Next row: K25, turn.

Next row: P24, turn.

Next row: K23, turn.

Next row: P22, turn.

Next row: K21, turn.

Next row: P20, turn.

Next row: K19, turn.

Next row: P18, turn.

Next row: K17, turn.

Next row: P16, turn.

Next row: K15, turn.

Next row: P14, turn.

Next row: K13, turn.

Next row: P12, turn.

Next row: K11, turn.

Next row: P10, turn.

Next row: K9, turn.

Next row: P8, turn.

Next row: K to end.

Next row: P to end.

Next row: K2, [k2tog, k3] to last 3 sts, k2tog, k1. (48 sts.)

P 1 row.

Next row: K14, k2tog, k2, [k2tog, k3] twice, k2tog, k2, k2tog, k14. (43 sts.)

P 1 row.

Next row: K14, [k2tog, k2] 3 times, k2tog, k15. (39 sts.)

Above: *the unicorn's mane flops between its ears*

P 1 row.

Beg with a k row, work 12 rows in st st.

Next row: K7, skpo, k1, skpo, k15, k2tog, k1, k2tog, k7. (35 sts.)

P 1 row.

Next row: K1, [k2tog] to end. (18 sts.)

Next row: [P2tog] to end. (9 sts.)

Bind off.

EARS (Make 2 Lilac, 2 White)

With US 2/3 (3 mm) needles and Lilac, cast on 8 sts.

Beg with a k row, work 8 rows in st st.

Dec 1 st at each end of next 3 rows. (2 sts.)

Bind off.

HORN

With US 2/3 (3 mm) needles and White, cast on
20 sts.
Beg with a k row, work 4 rows in st st.
Beg with a k row, work 18 rows in st st, dec 1 st at each end
of the next and foll alt rows. (2 sts.)
Bind off.

TO MAKE UP

Sew one end and underside seam of body. Stuff firmly.
Tail: Cut 20 x 6 in. (15 cm) lengths of Denim Ultra, and tie a
length of yarn around at one end to form a bunch. Place the
tied end in the open end of the body piece and close the
opening, catching in the bunch of yarn as you go. Join seam
of neck and chin of head piece, then the nose seam. Stuff
firmly, then sew to body. Sew each leg seam and then sew a
leg base in white end of each leg. Stuff each leg firmly and

sew each one to the body.
Sew the long seam of the horn together and stuff. Wrap yarn
around horn to form a spiral effect. Sew horn to center front
of head.
Sew one White and one Lilac ear together for each ear and
then sew to head either side of horn.
Mane: Cut 16 x 8 in. (20 cm) lengths of Denim Ultra and
place each piece of yarn on back of head and down neck.
Sew through, halfway along each piece, to back of head.
Embroider eyes and nostrils in satin stitch using black
embroidery thread. Sew eyelashes in black using straight
stitches. Sew mouth in stem stitch in black. Sew a small
white highlight in each eye.

Below: *underside of unicorn, showing leg construction*

Upside Down Dolly

Every little girl loves the Cinderella story, and this sweet little doll magically changes from her rags dress to her glittering gown just in time for the ball!

MEASUREMENTS
Approximately 10 in. (25 cm) tall

MATERIALS
- 1 x 100 g ball of King Cole Woolmix DK in Pink 6
- 1 x 100 g ball of King Cole Woolmix DK in Lilac 17
- 1 x 100 g ball of King Cole Big Value Baby DK in Jeans 207
- 1 x 100 g ball of King Cole Big Value DK in Dusky Pink 94
- 1 x 100 g ball of King Cole Woolmix DK in Beige 57
- 1 x 100 g ball of King Cole Petal DK in White 1
- Small amounts of DK yarn in Yellow and Red
- Pair of US 2/3 (3 mm) (use either US 2 or US 3, based on your gauge) knitting needles and 3 mm crochet hook
- Stranded embroidery thread in Black, White, Flesh tone and Pink
- Washable toy stuffing
- 1 x skein each of DMC Light effects embroidery thread in E316 Metallic Pink and E3852 Metallic Gold

ABBREVIATIONS
See page 10.

GAUGE
All above yarns
25 sts and 34 rows to 4 in. (10 cm) measured over stockinette stitch using US 2/3 (3 mm) needles.

DOLLS

BALLGOWN DOLLY HEAD & BODY
With US 2/3 (3 mm) needles and Pink, cast on 6 sts.
Next row: K, inc into every st. (12 sts.)
P 1 row.
Next row: K, inc into every st. (24 sts.)
P 1 row.
Next row: K1, inc into every foll st to last st, k1. (46 sts.)
Beg with a p row, work 15 rows in st st.
Shape neck
Next row: K1, [k2tog] to last st, k1. (24 sts.)
P 1 row.
Change to White.

Next row: K1, inc into every foll st to last st, k1. (46 sts.)
Beg with a p row, work 3 rows in st st.
Change to Dusky Pink, and beg with a k row, work 18 rows in st st.

RAGS DRESS DOLLY BODY & HEAD
Change to Lilac, and beg with a k row, work 20 rows in st st.
Next row: K1, [k2tog] to last st, k1. (24 sts.)
P 1 row.
Change to Pink.
Next row: K1, inc into every foll st to last st, k1. (46 sts.)
Beg with a p row, work 15 rows in st st.
Next row: K1, [k2tog] to last st, k1. (24 sts.)
P 1 row.
Next row: [K2tog] to end. (12 sts.)

Next row: [P2tog] to end. (6 sts.)

Break yarn (leaving a long length for making up), thread through rem 6 sts and draw up tightly.

BALLGOWN DOLLY ARMS (Make 2)

With US 2/3 (3 mm) needles and Dusky Pink, cast on 14 sts.

Next row: K, inc into every st. (28 sts.)

Beg with a p row, work 9 rows in st st.

Next row: [K2tog] to end. (14 sts.)

Change to White and beg with a p row, work 3 rows in st st.

Change to Pink and beg with a k row, work 12 rows in st st.

Next row: [K2tog] to end. (7 sts.)

Next row: P1, [p2tog] to end. (4 sts.)

Break yarn, thread through rem 4 sts and draw up tightly.

RAGS DRESS DOLLY ARMS (Make 2)

With US 2/3 (3 mm) needles and Lilac, cast on 14 sts.

Beg with a k row, work 20 rows in st st.

Change to Pink and beg with a k row, work 6 rows in st st.

Next row: [K2tog] to end. (7 sts.)

Next row: P1, [p2tog] to end. (4 sts.)

Break yarn, thread through rem 4 sts and draw up tightly.

CLOTHES

BALLGOWN DOLLY SKIRT

With US 2/3 (3 mm) needles and White, cast on 96 sts.

Beg with a k row, work 6 rows in st st.

Change to Dusky Pink.

Next row: [K7, sl 1] to last 8 sts, k8.

Next row: P8, [sl 1, p7] to end.

Rep the last 2 rows once more.

Beg with a k row, work 36 rows in st st.

Next row: [K2tog] to end. (48 sts.)

P 1 row.

Bind off.

RAGS DRESS DOLLY SKIRT

With US 2/3 (3 mm) needles and Jeans, cast on 96 sts.

Beg with a k row, work 46 rows in st st.

Next row: [K2tog] to end. (48 sts.)

P 1 row.

Bind off.

APRON

With US 2/3 (3 mm) needles and Beige, cast on 22 sts.

K 3 rows.

Next row: K2, p to last 2 sts, k2.

Keeping the 2 sts at each edge in g st throughout, work 22 rows.

Next row: K1, [k2tog] to last st, k1. (12 sts.)

Keeping the 2 sts at each edge in g st throughout, work 12 rows.

K 2 rows.

Bind off.

PATCHES (Make 2)

With US 2/3 (3 mm) needles and Red, cast on 10 sts.

Beg with a k row, work 14 rows in st st.

Bind off.

TO MAKE UP

Sew head and body seam of each doll, leaving an opening for stuffing. Stuff each head firmly. Run a draw thread of yarn

Left: *the ballgown skirt has embroidered flowers*

Right: *the rags dress doll has a simple dress and apron*

P 1 row.

Bind off.

FACE

With US 7 (4½ mm) needles and Orange, cast on 13 sts.

Beg with a k row, work 6 rows in st st.

Dec 1 st at each end of foll 2 rows. (9 sts.)

Bind off.

MUZZLE

With US 7 (4½ mm) needles and Orange, cast on 46 sts.

Beg with a k row, work 8 rows in st st.

Next row: K1, [k2tog, k4] 7 times, k2tog, k1. (38 sts.)

P 1 row.

Next row: K1, [k2tog, k3] 7 times, k2tog, k1. (30 sts.)

P 1 row.

Next row: [K2tog, k2] 7 times, k2tog. (22 sts.)

P 1 row.

Bind off.

EARS (Make 2 Red, 2 Orange)

With US 7 (4½ mm) needles, cast on 8 sts.

Beg with a k row, work 7 rows in st st.

Dec 1 st at each end of next 3 rows. (2 sts.)

Bind off.

ARMS (Make 2)

With 4½ mm (UK 7/US 7) needles and Red, cast on 19 sts.

Beg with a k row, work 48 rows in st st.

Bind off.

HANDS (Make 2))

With US 7 (4½ mm) needles and Orange, and with the p side of Arm facing, pick up and k 19 sts along cast-off edge.

P 1 row.

Shape thumb

Next row: K9, m1, k1, m1, k9. (21 sts.)

P 1 row.

Next row: K9, m1, k3, m1, k9. (23 sts.)

P 1 row.

Next row: K1, m1, k8, m1, k5, m1, k8, m1, k1. (27 sts.)

P 1 row.

Next row: K1, m1, k9, m1, k7, m1, k9, m1, k1. (31 sts.)

P 1 row.

Beg with a k row, work 2 rows in st st.

Next row: K19, turn.

Next row: P8, turn.

Work on these 8 sts only as follows:

Beg with a k row, work 2 rows in st st.

Next row: [K2tog] to end. (4 sts.)

Break yarn, thread through rem sts, draw up tightly and fasten off.

Shape hand

With RS facing, rejoin yarn to rem sts and k across 11 sts of hand, then 12 sts of other side of hand. (23 sts.)

P 1 row.

Next row: K1, [k2tog] to end. (12 sts.)

Next row: [P2tog] to end. (6 sts.)

Break yarn, thread through rem sts, draw up tightly and fasten off.

LEGS (Make 2)

With US 7 (4½ mm) needles and Red, cast on 21 sts.

Beg with a k row, work 54 rows in st st.

Bind off.

FEET (Make 2)

With US 7 (4½ mm) needles and Orange, and with the p side of Leg facing, pick up and k 21 sts along cast-off edge.

P 1 row.

Shape toe

Next row: K10, m1, k1, m1, k10. (23 sts.)

P 1 row.

Next row: K10, m1, k3, m1, k10. (25 sts.)

P 1 row.

Next row: K1, m1, k9, m1, k5, m1, k9, m1, k1. (29 sts.)

P 1 row.

Next row: K1, m1, k10, m1, k7, m1, k10, m1, k1. (33 sts.)

P 1 row.

Next row: K1, m1, k11, m1, k9, m1, k11, m1, k1. (37 sts.)

P 1 row.

Next row: K23, turn.

Next row: P10, turn.

Work on these 10 sts only as follows:

Beg with a k row, work 2 rows in st st.

Next row: [K2tog] to end. (5 sts.)

Break yarn, thread through rem sts, draw up tightly and fasten off.

Shape foot

With RS facing, rejoin yarn to rem sts and k across 13 sts of foot, then 14 sts of other side of foot. (27 sts.)
P 1 row.
Next row: K1, [k2tog] to end. (14 sts.)
P 1 row.
Next row: [K2tog] to end. (7 sts.)
Break yarn, thread through rem sts, draw up tightly and fasten off.

TAIL

With US 7 (4½ mm) needles and Red, cast on 8 sts.
K 1 row, turn and sl all sts back onto the right needle.
Turn again, and pulling the yarn tight from the left side,
k across the 8 sts. In this way you will k all rows and the row ends will pull together to make a tube.
Cont in this way until the tail measures 8½ in. (22 cm).
Break yarn, thread through sts, draw up tightly and fasten off.

FELTING INSTRUCTIONS

Work in all ends with a needle.
Following the instructions on page 17 for machine felting, felt all pieces in the washing machine on a 140°F (60°C) wash.
Reshape while damp, and dry thoroughly.

TO MAKE UP

Please note: With the exception of the tail, the purl/reverse side of all Red pieces is the right side. The knit side of all Orange pieces is the right side.
Join each leg, toe and foot seam. Stuff firmly and oversew top edges together.
Sew center back seam of body.
Place the oversewn ends of the legs at the bottom edge of the body and sew the seam together through all thicknesses.
Stuff the body firmly and oversew the top edge together.
Sew the center back seam of head. Sew bottom seam, stuff firmly and sew top seam. Sew to body.
Sew ends of muzzle together and then the nose seam. Stuff lightly. Sew face piece to head. Then position muzzle over the bottom edge of the face piece and sew to head.
Sew one Orange and one Red ear together for each ear. Sew to sides of head.
Sew thumb, hand and seam of each arm. Stuff firmly and sew to sides of body.
Sew tail to center back bottom.
Embroider eyes in satin stitch using black embroidery thread. Sew a small white highlight in each eye. Embroider mouth in stem stitch using black embroidery thread.

SCARF

With US 6 (4 mm) needles and Indigo, cast on 105 sts.
Working in g st throughout and 2 rows Indigo, 2 rows Cornflower, work 14 rows.
Bind off.

Please note: Scarf is not felted.
Fringing: Cut 16 x 4 in. (10 cm) lengths of Indigo yarn and 12 x 4 in. (10 cm) lengths of Cornflower yarn. Take two lengths and knot through the corresponding colored stripes at each end of the scarf.

Left: funky monkey in his extra long scarf

Fluffy Puppy

Everyone's best friend; Fluffy Puppy could be a first pet for a child. His intarsia spots add to his cuteness and he is the perfect size to tuck under a child's arm.

felted knitting

★
★
★

SKILL LEVEL:
advanced

MEASUREMENTS
Approximately 10 in. (25 cm) long

MATERIALS
- 2 x 50 g balls of Alpaca Select 100% Alpaca DK in Cream 1
- 1 x 50 g ball of Alpaca Select 100% Alpaca DK in Brown 4
- 1 x 50 g ball of Alpaca Select 100% Alpaca DK in Tan 2
- Oddments of Alpaca Select 100% Alpaca DK in Red 17
- Pair each of US 7 (4½ mm) and US 6 (4 mm) knitting needles
- Stranded embroidery thread in Black and White
- Washable toy stuffing

ABBREVIATIONS
See page 10.

GAUGE
20 sts and 25 rows to 4 in. (10 cm) measured over stockinette stitch using US 7 (4½ mm) needles before machine felting.

PUPPY

LEFT SIDE BODY
Front leg

With US 7 (4½ mm) needles and Cream, cast on 14 sts.
Beg with a k row, work 8 rows in st st.
Using the intarsia method, cont as follows:
Row 9: K12 Cream, k2 Brown.
Row 10: P4 Brown, p10 Cream.
Row 11: K8 Cream, k6 Brown.
Row 12: P7 Brown, p7 Cream.
Row 13: K6 Cream, k8 Brown.
Row 14: P8 Brown, p6 Cream .
Row 15: As Row 13.
Row 16: P9 Brown, p5 Cream.
Break yarn and place sts on a spare needle.

Back leg

With US 7 (4½ mm) needles and Cream, cast on 14 sts.
Beg with a k row, work 4 rows in st st.
Row 5: K6 Cream, k4 Brown, k4 Cream.
Row 6: P3 Cream, p6 Brown, p5 Cream.
Row 7: K4 Cream, k8 Brown, k2 Cream.
Row 8: P2 Cream, p8 Brown, p4 Cream.
Row 9: As Row 7.
Row 10: As Row 8.
Row 11: K5 Cream, k7 Brown, k2 Cream.
Row 12: P2 Cream, p7 Brown, p5 Cream.
Row 13: K6 Cream, k5 Brown, k3 Cream.
Row 14: P5 Cream, p2 Brown, p7 Cream .
Row 15: K3 Tan, k11 Cream.
Row 16: Cast on 12 sts, p22 Cream, p4 Tan.
Join legs
Row 17: With RS facing, k5 Tan, k21 Cream of back leg, then k5 Cream, k9 Brown of front leg. (40 sts.)

Row 18: P9 Brown, p25 Cream, p6 Tan.

Row 19: K6 Tan, k25 Cream, k9 Brown.

Row 20: P8 Brown, p26 Cream, p6 Tan.

Row 21: K6 Tan, k17 Cream, k4 Tan, k5 Cream, k8 Brown.

Row 22: P7 Brown, p5 Cream, p6 Tan, p15 Cream, p7 Tan.

Row 23: K7 Tan, k15 Cream, k6 Tan, k6 Cream, k6 Brown.

Row 24: P5 Brown, p6 Cream, p8 Tan, p14 Cream, p7 Tan.

Row 25: K7 Tan, k14 Cream, k8 Tan, k7 Cream, k4 Brown.

Row 26: P3 Brown, p8 Cream, p8 Tan, p14 Cream, p7 Tan.

Row 27: K6 Tan, k15 Cream, k8 Tan, k11 Cream.

Row 28: P11 Cream, p7 Tan, p16 Cream, p6 Tan.

Row 29: K6 Tan, k17 Cream, k5 Tan, k12 Cream.

Row 30: Cast on 15 sts, p28 Cream, p3 Tan, p19 Cream, p5 Tan. (55 sts.)

Row 31: K4 Tan, k9 Cream, k5 Brown, k37 Cream.

Row 32: P35 Cream, p9 Brown, p8 Cream, p3 Tan.

Row 33: K10 Cream, k12 Brown, k33 Cream.

Row 34: P32 Cream, p14 Brown, p9 Cream.

Row 35: K8 Cream, k16 Brown, k31 Cream.

Row 36: P30 Cream, p17 Brown, p8 Cream.

Row 37: K7 Cream, k18 Brown, k6 Cream, k6 Tan, k18 Cream.

Row 38: P17 Cream, p8 Tan, p5 Cream, p18 Brown, p7 Cream.

Row 39: K7 Cream, k19 Brown, k3 Cream, k10 Tan, k16 Cream.

Row 40: P16 Cream, p10 Tan, p3 Cream, p19 Brown, p7 Cream.

Row 41: K6 Cream, cast off 25 sts, k9 Tan, k15 Cream. Working on these 24 sts of head only, cont as follows:

Row 42: P15 Cream, p9 Tan.

Row 43: K2tog Tan, k7 Tan, k15 Cream.

Row 44: P15 Cream, p8 Tan.

Row 45: K2tog Tan, k6 Tan, k13 Cream, k2tog Cream.

Row 46: Bind off 2 sts, p12 Cream, p7 Tan.

Row 47: K2tog Tan, K5 Tan, k12 Cream.

Row 48: Bind off 4 sts, p9 Cream, p5 Tan.

Row 49: K2tog Tan, k2 Tan, k10 Cream.

Row 50: Bind off 5 sts, p6 Cream, p2 Tan.

Row 51: K8 Cream.

Row 52: Bind off 3 sts, p5 Cream.

Row 53: K3, k2tog.

Row 54: P2tog, p2. (3 sts.)

Beg with a k row, work 2 rows in st st.

Bind off.

With WS facing, rejoin yarn to rem 6 sts for tail and cont as follows:

Beg with p row, work 15 rows, dec 1 st at inside edge of every 5th row. (3 sts.)
Bind off.

RIGHT SIDE BODY

Front leg

With US 7 (4½ mm) needles and Cream, cast on 14 sts.
Beg with a k row, work 8 rows in st st.
Using the intarsia method, cont as follows:

Row 9: K2 Brown, k12 Cream.
Row 10: P10 Cream, p4 Brown.
Row 11: K6 Brown, k8 Cream.
Row 12: P7 Cream, p7 Brown.
Row 13: K8 Brown, k6 Cream.
Row 14: P6 Cream, p8 Brown.
Row 15: As Row 13.
Row 16: P5 Cream, p9 Brown.
Break yarn and place sts on a spare needle.

Back leg

With US 7 (4½ mm) needles and Cream, cast on 14 sts.
Beg with a k row, work 4 rows in st st.

Row 5: K4 Cream, k4 Brown, k6 Cream.
Row 6: P5 Cream, p6 Brown, p3 Cream.
Row 7: K2 Cream, k8 Brown, k4 Cream.
Row 8: P4 Cream, p8 Brown, p2 Cream.
Row 9: As Row 7.
Row 10: As Row 8.
Row 11: K2 Cream, k7 Brown, k5 Cream.
Row 12: P5 Cream, p7 Brown, p2 Cream.
Row 13: K3 Cream, k5 Brown, k6 Cream.
Row 14: P7 Cream, p2 Brown, p5 Cream.
Row 15: K11 Cream, k3 Tan.
Row 16: P4 Tan, p10 Cream.
Turn and cast on 12 sts.

Join legs

Row 17: With RS facing, k9 Brown, k5 Cream of front leg, then k21 Cream, k5 Tan, of back leg. (40 sts.)
Row 18: P6 Tan, p25 Cream, p9 Brown.
Row 19: K9 Brown, k25 Cream, k6 Tan.
Row 20: P6 Tan, p26 Cream, p8 Brown.
Row 21: K8 Brown, k5 Cream, k4 Tan, k17 Cream, k6 Tan.
Row 22: P7 Tan, p15 Cream, p6 Tan, p5 Cream, p7 Brown.
Row 23: K6 Brown, k6 Cream, k6 Tan, k15 Cream, k7 Tan.
Row 24: P7 Tan, p14 Cream, p8 Tan, p6 Cream, p5 Brown.
Row 25: K4 Brown, k7 Cream, K8 Tan, k14 Cream, k7 Tan.
Row 26: P7 Tan, p14 Cream, p8 Tan, p8 Cream, p3 Brown.
Row 27: K11 Cream, k8 Tan, k15 Cream, k6 Tan.

Above: *Fluffy Puppy's markings, in Tan and Brown*

Row 28: P6 Tan, p16 Cream, p7 Tan, p11 Cream.
Row 29: K12 Cream, k5 Tan, k17 Cream, k6 Tan.
Row 30: P5 Tan, p19 Cream, p3 Tan, p13 Cream.
Row 31: Cast on 15 sts, k37 Cream, k5 Brown, k9 Cream, k4 Tan. (55 sts.)
Row 32: P3 Tan, p8 Cream, p9 Brown, p35 Cream.
Row 33: K33 Cream, k12 Brown, k10 Cream.
Row 34: P9 Cream, p14 Brown, p32 Cream.
Row 35: K31 Cream, k16 Brown, k8 Cream.
Row 36: P8 Cream, p17 Brown, p30 Cream.
Row 37: K18 Cream, k6 Tan, k6 Cream, k18 Brown, k7 Cream.
Row 38: P7 Cream, p18 Brown, p5 Cream, p8 Tan, p17 Cream.
Row 39: K16 Cream, k10 Tan, k3 Cream, k19 Brown, k7 Cream.
Row 40: P7 Cream, p19 Brown, p3 Cream, p10 Tan, p16 Cream.
Row 41: K15 Cream, k9 Tan, cast off 25 sts, k6 Cream.
Working on these 6 sts of tail only, cont as follows:
Beg with p row, work 15 rows, dec 1 st at inside edge of every 5th row. (3 sts.)

Bind off.

With WS facing, rejoin yarn to rem 24 sts for head and cont as follows:

Row 42: P9 Tan, p15 Cream.

Row 43: K15 Cream, k7 Tan, k2tog. (23 sts.)

Row 44: P8 Tan, p15 Cream.

Row 45: K2tog Cream, k13 Cream, k6 Tan, k2tog.

Row 46: P7 Tan, p14 Cream.

Row 47: Bind off 2 sts, k12 Cream, k5 Tan, k2tog.

Row 48: P5 Tan, p13 Cream.

Row 49: Bind off 4 sts, k10 Cream, k2 Tan, k2tog.

Row 50: P2 Tan, p11 Cream.

Row 51: Bind off 5 sts, k8 Cream.

Row 52: P8 Cream.

Row 53: Bind off 3 sts, k5.

Row 54: P5.

Row 55: Bind off 2 sts, k3.

Row 56: P3.

Bind off.

BODY GUSSET

With US 7 (4½ mm) needles and Cream, cast on 2 sts.

Beg with a k row, work 6 rows in st st, inc 1 st at each end of every alt row. (8 sts.)

Beg with a k row, work 24 rows in st st.

Cast on 14 sts at beg of next 2 rows. (36 sts.)

Beg with a k row, work 16 rows in st st.

Bind off 12 sts at beg of next 2 rows. (12 sts.)

Beg with a k row, work 14 rows in st st.

Cast on 12 sts at beg of next 2 rows. (36 sts.)

Beg with a k row, work 16 rows in st st.

Bind off 15 sts at beg of next 2 rows. (6 sts.)

Beg with a k row, work 6 rows in st st, dec 1 st at each end of every 3rd row. (2 sts.)

Bind off.

HEAD GUSSET

With US 7 (4½ mm) needles and Cream, cast on 2 sts.

Beg with a k row, work 8 rows in st st, inc 1 st at each end of every 4th row. (6 sts.)

Beg with a k row, work 16 rows in st st.

Beg with a k row, work 3 rows in st st, inc 1 st at each end of every row. (12 sts.)

P1 row.

K 1 row.

Beg with a p row, work 3 rows in st st, dec 1 st at each end of every row. (6 sts.)

Beg with a k row, work 8 rows in st st, dec 1 st at each end of every foll 3rd row. (2 sts.)

Bind off.

FELTING INSTRUCTIONS

Work in all ends with a needle.

Following the instructions on page 17 for machine felting, felt all pieces in the washing machine on a 140°F (60°C) wash. Reshape while damp, and dry thoroughly.

TO MAKE UP

Stitch head gusset between ears on each head piece, sewing the long end down towards the nose.

Sew center back seam of body pieces.

Sew body gusset to legs and lower body, leaving the tail end open for stuffing. Stuff firmly and close opening.

Embroider eyes and nose in satin stitch, using black embroidery thread. Embroider mouth in stem stitch using black embroidery thread. Sew a small white highlight in each eye.

COLLAR

With US 6 (4 mm) needles and Red, cast on 30 sts.

K 2 rows.

Bind off.

Wrap collar around neck of dog and join ends.

Below: *detail showing head gussett*

Ellie Flowers

A fun, felted, pink elephant, sprinkled in pretty flowers. A charming companion for your little one's trip to the zoo.

felted knitting

★
★
★

SKILL LEVEL:
advanced

MEASUREMENTS
Approximately 8 in. (20 cm) tall

MATERIALS
- 2 x 50 g balls of Alpaca Select 100% Alpaca DK in Pink 37
- 1 x 50 g ball of Alpaca Select 100% Alpaca DK in Purple 36
- 1 x 50 g ball of Alpaca Select 100% Alpaca DK in Lilac 29
- 1 x 50 g ball of Alpaca Select 100% Alpaca DK in Burgundy 38
- Oddments of Alpaca Select 100% Alpaca DK in Green 22
- Pair of US 7 (4½ mm) knitting needles
- Stranded embroidery thread in Black
- Washable toy stuffing

ABBREVIATIONS
See page 10.

GAUGE
20 sts and 25 rows to 4 in. (10 cm) measured over stockinette stitch using US 7 (4½ mm) needles before hand felting.

ELEPHANT

LEFT SIDE BODY
Front leg
* With US 7 (4½ mm) needles and Pink, cast on 10 sts.
K 1 row.
Beg with a p row, work 3 rows in st st, at the same time, inc 1 st at each end of the next 2 rows. (14 sts.) *

Place flower
Next row: K3, k across 9 sts of Row 1 of Chart A, k2.
Beg with a p row, and using the intarsia method, work the rem 11 rows of the chart in st st, inc 1 st at end of final row. (15 sts.)
Next row: K all sts in Pink.
Next row: P 1 row inc 1 st at end of row. (16 sts.)
Break yarn and place sts on a spare needle.

Back leg
Work as for front leg from * to *.

Place flower
Next row: K2, k across 9 sts of Row 1 of Chart B, k3.
Beg with a p row, and using the intarsia method, work the rem 11 rows of the chart in st st, inc 1 st at beg of final row. (15 sts.)
Next row: K all sts in Pink.
Next row: P 1 row inc 1 st at beg of row. (16 sts.)
Join legs
Next row: K across 16 sts of back leg, turn and cast on 4 sts, turn again and with RS facing, k across 16 sts of front leg. (36 sts.)
P 1 row.

Place two flowers
Next row: K4, k across 25 sts of Row 1 of Chart C, k7.
Beg with a p row, and using the intarsia method, work 4 rows of the chart in st st.

Next row: Working Row 6 of Chart C, inc 1 st at end of row.
(37 sts.)
Break yarn and place sts on a spare needle.

TAIL

With US 7 (4½ mm) needles and Pink, cast on 3 sts.
Beg with a k row, work 2 rows in st st.

Beg with a k row, work 2 rows in st st, at the same time
inc 1 st at end of each row. (5 sts.)
Beg with a k row, work 2 rows in st st.
Next row: K, inc 1 st at end of row. (6 sts.)
Beg with a p row, work 3 rows in st st.
Next row: K, inc 1 st at end of row. (7 sts.)
P 1 row.

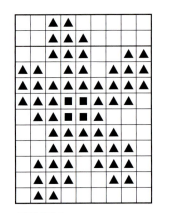

CHART A

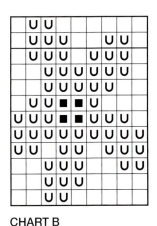

CHART B

KEY

☐	Pink
■	Green
−	Burgundy
▲	Purple
U	Lilac

CHART C

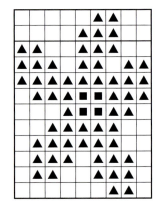

CHART D

CHART E

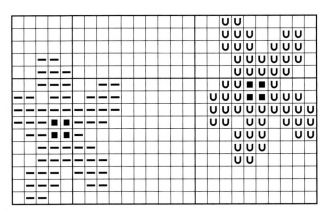

CHART F

Left: *detail showing tail and saddle*

Next row: K2tog, k to end. (7 sts.)

P 1 row.

Next row: K to last st, inc 1. (8 sts.)

Next row: P to last 2 sts, p2tog. (7 sts.)

K 1 row.

Next row: Inc 1 st, p to end. (8 sts.)

Beg with a k row, work 3 rows in st st.

Next row: P to last st, inc 1. (9 sts.)

K 1 row.

Next row: P to last st, inc 1. (10 sts.)

Next row: Cast on 3 sts, break yarn and place these 13 sts on a spare needle.

Join to body

With RS facing, rejoin yarn to body and k across 46 sts of tail and body (still working the rem rows of Chart C), then 13 sts of trunk. (59 sts.)

Beg with a p row, work 7 rows in st st completing rem rows of Chart C.

Place final flower

Next row: K7, k across 9 sts of Row 1 of Chart A, k to last 2 sts, k2tog. (58 sts.)

Beg with a p row, and using the intarsia method, work 2 rows of the chart in st st.

Cont to complete Chart A, at the same time dec as follows:

Next row: P to last 2 sts, p2tog.

K 1 row.

Next row: P2tog, p to end.

Beg with a k row, work 2 rows in st st.

Next row: Dec 1 st at each end of row.

P 1 row.

Rep the last 2 rows once more.

Dec 1 st at each end of next 2 rows.

Next row: K2tog, k to end.

Next row: Dec 1 st at each end of row.

Next row: Bind off 2 sts, k to last 2 sts, k2tog.

Next row: P2tog, p to end.

Next row: Bind off 2 sts, k to last 2 sts, k2tog.

Next row: Dec 1 st at each end of row.

Next row: Bind off 5 sts, k to last 2 sts, k2tog.

Next row: Bind off 2 sts, p to end.

Next row: Bind off 5 sts, k to last 2 sts, k2tog.

Next row: Bind off 3 sts, p to end.

Bind off rem 19 sts.

Join to body

Next row: K across 7 sts of tail, then inc in 1st st of body and k across rem 36 sts of body (still working the rem rows from Chart C), inc 1 st at end of row. (46 sts.)

P 1 row.

Break yarn and place sts on a spare needle.

TRUNK

With US 7 (4½ mm) needles and Pink, cast on 3 sts.

K 1 row.

Beg with a p row, work 2 rows in st st, at the same time inc 1 st at each end of both rows. (7 sts.)

P 1 row.

Next row: K, inc 1 st at end of row. (8 sts.)

P 1 row.

Next row: K2tog, k to last st, inc 1.

P 1 row.

RIGHT SIDE BODY

Front leg

** With US 7 (4½ mm) needles and Pink, cast on
10 sts.

K 1 row.

Beg with a p row, work 3 rows in st st, at the same time, inc
1 st at each end of the next 2 rows. (14 sts.) **

Place flower

Next row: K2, k across 9 sts of Row 1 of Chart D, k3.

Beg with a p row, and using the intarsia method, work the
rem 11 rows of the chart in st st, inc 1 st at beg of final row.
(15 sts.)

Next row: K all sts in Pink.

Next row: P 1 row inc 1 st at beg of row. (16 sts.)

Break yarn and place sts on a spare needle.

Back leg

Work as for front leg from ** to **.

Place flower

Next row: K3, k across 9 sts of Row 1 of Chart E, k2.

Beg with a p row, and using the intarsia method, work the
rem 11 rows of the chart in st st, inc 1 st at end of final row.
(15 sts.)

Next row: K all sts in Pink.

Next row: P 1 row inc 1 st at end of row. (16 sts.)

Turn and cast on 4 sts. (20 sts.)

Break yarn and place sts on a spare needle.

Join legs

Next row: With RS facing and Pink, k across 16 sts of front
leg, and k across 20 sts of back leg. (36 sts.)

P 1 row.

Place two flowers

Next row: K7, k across 25 sts of Row 1 of Chart F, k4.

Beg with a p row, and using the intarsia method, work 4
rows of the chart in st st.

Next row: Working Row 6 of Chart F, inc 1 st at beg of row.
(37 sts.)

Break yarn and place sts on a spare needle.

Below: *the felted knitting creates a lovely soft toy*

TAIL

With US 7 (4½ mm) needles and Pink, cast on 3 sts.

Beg with a k row, work 2 rows in st st.

Beg with a k row, work 2 rows in st st, at the same time inc 1 st at beg of both rows. (5 sts.)

Beg with a k row, work 2 rows in st st.

Next row: K, inc 1 st at beg of row. (6 sts.)

Beg with a p row, work 3 rows in st st.

Next row: K, inc 1 st at beg of row. (7 sts.)

P 1 row.

Join to body

Next row: Inc in the 1st st, k across 37 sts of body (still working the rem rows from Chart F), then inc in 1st st of tail and k rem 6 sts of tail. (46 sts.)

P 1 row.

Break yarn and place sts on a spare needle.

TRUNK

With US 7 (4½ mm) needles and Pink, cast on 3 sts.

K 1 row.

Beg with a p row, work 2 rows in st st, at the same time inc 1 st at each end of both rows. (7 sts.)

P 1 row.

Next row: K, inc 1 st at beg of row. (8 sts.)

P 1 row.

Next row: Inc 1, k to last 2 sts, k2tog.

P 1 row.

Next row: K to last 2 sts, k2tog. (7 sts.)

P 1 row.

Next row: Inc 1, k to end. (8 sts.)

Next row: P2tog, p to end. (7 sts.)

K 1 row.

Next row: P to last st, inc 1. (8 sts.)

Beg with a k row, work 3 rows in st st.

Next row: Inc 1, p to end. (9 sts.)

K 1 row.

Next row: Inc 1, p to end. (10 sts.)

Join to body

With RS facing, k across 10 sts of trunk, turn and cast on 3 sts, turn again and k across 46 sts of body and tail (still working the rem rows of Chart F). (59 sts.)

Beg with a p row, work 7 rows in st st completing rem rows of Chart F.

Place final flower

Next row: K2tog, k41, k across 9 sts of Row 1 of Chart D, k7.

Beg with a p row, and using the intarsia method, work 2 rows of the chart in st st.

Cont to complete Chart D, at the same time dec as follows.

Next row: P2tog, p to end.

K 1 row.

Next row: P to last 2 sts, p2tog.

Beg with a k row, work 2 rows in st st.

Next row: Dec 1 st at each end of row.

P 1 row.

Rep the last 2 rows once more.

Dec 1 st at each end of next 2 rows.

Next row: K to last 2 sts, k2tog.

Next row: Dec 1 st at each end of row.

Next row: K2tog, k to end.

Next row: Bind off 2 sts, p to last 2 sts, p2tog.

Next row: K2tog, k to end.

Next row: Bind off 2 sts, p to last 2 sts, p2tog

Next row: K2tog, k to end.

Next row: Bind off 5 sts, p to last 2 sts, p2tog.

Next row: Bind off 2 sts, k to end.

Next row: Bind off 5 sts, p to last 2 sts, p2tog.

Next row: Bind off 3 sts, k to end.

Bind off rem 19 sts.

GUSSET

Front leg

*** With US 7 (4½ mm) needles and Pink, cast on 10 sts.

K 1 row.

Beg with a p row, work 2 rows in st st, at the same time, inc 1 st at each end of both rows. (14 sts.)

Beg with a p row, work 12 rows in st st. ***

Next row: P, inc 1 st at beg of row.

K 1 row.

Next row: P, inc 1 st at beg of row. (16 sts.)

Break yarn and place sts on a spare needle.

Back leg

Work as for front leg from *** to ***.

Next row: P, inc 1 st at end of row.

K 1 row.

Next row: P, inc 1 st at end of row. (16 sts.)

Turn and cast on 4 sts. (20 sts.)

Break yarn and place sts on a spare needle.

Join legs

With RS facing and Pink, k across 16 sts of front leg and 20 sts of back leg. (36 sts.)

Beg with a p row, work 5 rows in st st, at the same time, inc 1 st at each end of every row. (46 sts.)

K 1 row.

Above: detail showing face, ears and trunk

Beg with a p row, work 5 rows in st st, at the same time, dec 1 st at each end of every row. (36 sts.)

Divide for legs

Next row: K16, turn.

Work on these 16 sts only as follows:

Next row: P2tog, p to end.

K 1 row.

Next row: P2tog, p to end. (14 sts.)

**** Beg with a k row, work 12 rows in st st.

Dec 1 st at each end of the next 2 rows. (10 sts.)

Bind off. ****

With RS facing and Pink, rejoin yarn to rem sts and work as follows:

Next row: Bind off 4 sts, k to end. (16 sts.)

Next row: P to last 2 sts, p2tog.

K 1 row.

Next row: P to last 2 sts, p2tog.

Work as for first leg from **** to ****.

EARS (Make 2)

With US 7 (4½ mm) needles and Pink, cast on 11 sts.

Beg with a k row, work 2 rows in st st.

Next row: Inc 1 st at each end of row.

P 1 row.

Rep the last 2 rows, twice more. (17 sts.)

Next row: Dec 1 st at each end of row.

P 1 row.

Rep the last 2 rows, once more. (13 sts.)

Bind off.

SADDLE

With US 7 (4½ mm) needles and Lilac, cast on 5 sts.

K 2 rows.

Next row: K2, m1, k to last 2 sts, m1, k2.

Next row: K2, p to last 2 sts, k2.

Keeping the 2 sts at either edge in g st on every row, work stripes of 2 rows Pink, 2 rows Green, 4 rows Lilac, and inc on every 3rd row to 15 sts.

Then inc 1 st at each end of every alt row to 19 sts.

Work 4 rows in st st, still keeping the edges in g st.

Next row: K2, k2tog, k to last 4 sts, k2tog, k2.

Next row: K2, p to last 2 sts, k2.

Rep the last 2 rows once more.

Then dec at each end of every 3rd row until 5 sts rem.

K 2 rows.

Bind off.

FELTING INSTRUCTIONS

Work in all ends with a needle.

Following the instructions on page 17 for hand felting, felt all pieces for approximately 30 minutes.

Reshape while damp, and dry thoroughly.

TO MAKE UP

With right sides together, sew the gusset to the corresponding legs, and the points along the edges under the tail and trunk.

Sew left and right side pieces together, curving the seam to follow the shaping and leaving an opening at the top of the back.

Turn right side out and push out all seams. Stuff firmly and close opening.

Attach ears at either side of head, and stitch saddle to back.

Embroider eyes either side of head using black embroidery thread and satin stitch.

Builder Ben

Builder Ben, with his hard hat and tool belt is just perfect for any budding construction workers. Without his hat, tool belt and boots, he's a cute little boy in his dungarees, ready to play.

MEASUREMENTS
Approximately 13 in. (33 cm) tall

MATERIALS
- 1 x 100 g ball of King Cole Big Value Baby DK in Taupe 37
- 1 x 100 g ball of King Cole Woolmix DK in White 1
- 1 x 50 g ball of King Cole Woolmix DK in Denim 96
- Small amounts of DK yarn in Yellow, Brown, Beige, Grey and Black
- Pair of US 2/3 (3 mm) (use either US 2 or US 3, based on your gauge)

knitting needles
- Stranded embroidery thread in Black, White, Flesh tone and Pink
- Washable toy stuffing
- 1 x press stud fastener

ABBREVIATIONS
See page 10.

GAUGE
Woolmix DK and Big Value Baby DK
25 sts and 34 rows to 4 in. (10 cm) measured over stockinette stitch using US 2/3 (3 mm) needles.

BOY DOLL

BODY & HEAD
With US 2/3 (3 mm) needles and Denim, cast on 53 sts.
Beg with a k row, work 14 rows in st st.
Next row (RS): P.
Next row: K.
Change to White and beg with a k row, work 20 rows in st st.
Shape shoulders
Next row: K13, skpo, k23, k2tog, k13. (51 sts.)
P 1 row.
Next row: K13, skpo, k21, k2tog, k13. (49 sts.)
P 1 row.
Next row: K12, skpo, k21, k2tog, k12. (47 sts.)
P 1 row.
Next row: K1, [k2tog] to last 2 sts, k2. (25 sts.)
P 1 row.

Change to Taupe and beg with a k row, work 2 rows in st st.
Shape head
Next row: K1, [k1, m1] to last st, k1. (48 sts.)
P 1 row.
Next row: K13, m1, k22, m1, k13. (50 sts.)
P 1 row.
Next row: K13, m1, k1, m1, k22, m1, k1, m1, k13. (54 sts.)
Beg with a p row, work 21 rows in st st.
Shape top of head
Next row: [K2, k2tog] to last 2 sts, k2. (41 sts.)
P 1 row.
Next row: K1, [k2tog] to last 2 sts, k2. (22 sts.)
P 1 row.
Next row: [K2tog] to end. (11 sts.)
Next row: [P2tog] to last st, p1.
Break yarn (leaving a long length for making up), thread through rem 6 sts and draw up tightly.

BODY BASE

With US 2/3 (3 mm) needles and Denim, cast on 10 sts.

Beg with a k row, work 2 rows in st st.

Next row: Cast on 2 sts, k to end.

Next row: Cast on 2 sts, p to end.

Rep the last 2 rows once more. (18 sts.)

Next row: Inc 1, k to last st, inc 1.

P 1 row.

Rep the last 2 rows once more. (22 sts.)

Work 2 rows in st st.

Next row: Skpo, k18, k2tog. (20 sts.)

P 1 row.

Next row: Skpo, k16, k2tog. (18 sts.)

Next row: Bind off 2 sts, p to end.

Next row: Bind off 2 sts, k to end.

Rep the last 2 rows once more. (10 sts.)

P 1 row.

Bind off.

LEGS (Make 2)

With US 2/3 (3 mm) needles and Denim, cast on
26 sts.

Beg with a k row, work 30 rows in st st.

Change to Taupe and beg with a k row, work 2 rows in st st.

Shape instep

Next row: K16, turn.

Next row: P6, turn.

Working on these 6 sts only, work 8 rows in st st.

Break yarn and leave these sts on a spare needle.

With RS facing, rejoin yarn at base of instep and k up 7 sts
down side of instep, k6 sts from spare needle, k up 7 sts up
other side of instep and k rem 10 sts. (40 sts.)

Beg with a p row, work 3 rows in st st.

Shape sole

Next row: K1, skpo, k13, skpo, k4, k2tog, k13, k2tog, k1.
(36 sts.)

P 1 row.

Next row: K1, skpo, k12, skpo, k2, k2tog, k12, k2tog, k1.
(32 sts.)

P 1 row

Next row: K1, [k2tog] to last st, k1. (17 sts.)

P 1 row.

Bind off.

ARMS (Make 2)

With US 2/3 (3 mm) needles and White, cast on 6 sts.

Beg with a k row, work 2 rows in st st.

Next row: K1, m1, k to last st, m1, k1.

P 1 row.

Rep the last 2 rows until there are 18 sts.

Beg with a k row, work 2 rows in st st.

Change to Taupe and beg with a k row, work 16 rows
in st st.

Shape hand

Next row: K9, m1, k9. (19 sts.)

P 1 row.

Next row: K9, m1, k1, m1, k9. (21 sts.)

P 1 row.

Next row: K9, m1, k3, m1, k9. (23 sts.)

P 1 row.

Next row: K9, m1, k5, m1, k9. (25 sts.)

P 1 row.

Next row: K9, [skpo] twice, [k2tog] twice, k8. (21 sts.)

Next row: P8, [p2tog] twice, p9. (19 sts.)

Next row: K9, k2tog, k8. (18 sts.)

P 1 row.

Next row: K1, skpo, k4, [k2tog] twice, k4, k2tog, k1.
(14 sts.)

P 1 row.

Next row: K1, [k2tog] to last st, k1. (8 sts.)

Next row: [P2tog] 4 times.

Break yarn, thread through rem 4 sts and draw up tightly.

TO MAKE UP

Join center back seam of body and head. Attach body base
to bottom edges of body, leaving an opening for stuffing.
Stuff head firmly. Wind a length of White yarn quite tightly
around neck where the color changes and secure. Stuff
remainder of body and close opening.

Sew sole, heel and center back seam of each leg and stuff.
Sew legs to bottom of body, lining up outside edge of each
leg with edge of body.

Sew underarm seam of each arm. Stuff and sew to sides of
body over shoulder shaping.

Sew loops of Black yarn to head for hair, starting at front and
working towards crown.

Embroider eyes in satin stitch using black embroidery
thread. Sew a small white highlight in each eye. Work nose
and mouth in stem stitch, using flesh tone and pink
respectively.

CLOTHES AND TOOLS

DUNGAREE BIB

Front

With US 2/3 (3 mm) needles and Denim, cast on
12 sts.

Next row: K.

Next row: K2, p to last 2 sts, k2.

Rep last 2 rows 7 times more.

K 4 rows.

Bind off.

Back

With US 2/3 (3 mm) needles and Denim, cast on
6 sts.

Next row: K.

Next row: K2, p2, k2.

Rep the last 2 rows 6 times.

K 4 rows.

Divide for straps

Next row: K3, turn.

Working on these 3 sts only, cont in g st until strap measures
8 cm (3 in.) when slightly stretched.

Bind off.

Rejoin yarn to rem 3 sts and work as for first strap.

Sew bottom edge of each bib to front and back of doll.

Place straps over shoulders and tuck under front bib. Stitch
through all thicknesses using Grey yarn.

HAT

Crown

With US 2/3 (3 mm) needles and Yellow, cast on
55 sts.

Beg with a k row, work 4 rows in st st.

Next row: K2, [k2tog, k5] 7 times, k2tog, k2. (47 sts.)

P 1 row.

Next row: K1, [k2tog, k4] 7 times, k2tog, k2. (39 sts.)

P 1 row.

Next row: K1, [k2tog, k3] 7 times, k2tog, k1. (31 sts.)

P 1 row.

Next row: K1, [k2tog, k2] 7 times, k2. (24 sts.)

P 1 row.

Next row: [K2tog] to end. (12 sts.)

P 1 row.

Break yarn, thread through rem sts and pull up tightly.

Above: the hat, belt and boots can all be removed

Brim

With US 2/3 (3 mm) needles and Yellow, pick up and
k 53 sts along cast-on edge of hat crown.

Work in g st and cont thus:

K 1 row.

Bind off 11 sts at beg of next 2 rows. (31 sts.)

Bind off 6 sts at beg of next 2 rows. (19 sts.)

Bind off 4 sts at beg of next 2 rows. (11 sts.)

Next row: K1, [m1, k1] to end. (21 sts.)

K 1 row.

Dec 1 st at each end of next 4 rows. (13 sts.)

Bind off 4 sts at beg of next 2 rows.

Bind off rem 5 sts.

Sew seam of hat.

BOOTS (Make 2)

With US 2/3 (3 mm) needles and Brown, cast on
30 sts.

K 4 rows.

Beg with a k row, work 8 rows in st st.

Shape instep

Next row: K19, turn.

Next row: P8, turn.

Working on these 8 sts only, work 8 rows in st st.

Break yarn and leave these sts on a spare needle.

With RS facing, rejoin yarn at base of instep and k up 9 sts
down side of instep, k 8 sts from spare needle, k up 9 sts up
other side of instep and k rem 11 sts. (48 sts.)

Beg with a p row, work 3 rows in st st.

Change to Beige and beg with a k row, work 2 rows in st st.
Bind off.

Soles (Make 2)

With US 2/3 (3 mm) needles and Beige, cast on 6 sts.

Beg with a k row, work 2 rows in st st.

Next row: K1, m1, k to last st, m1, k1. (8 sts.)

Beg with a p row, work 14 rows in st st.

Next row: P2tog, p to last 2 sts, p2tog. (6 sts.)

Beg with a k row, work 2 rows in st st.

Bind off.

Sew center back seam of each boot, then sew a sole to the
bottom edge of each boot.

TOOL BELT

Belt

With US 2/3 (3 mm) needles and Brown, cast on 3 sts.

Work in g st until belt measures 25 cm (10 in.) when slightly
stretched.

Bind off.

Pocket

With US 2/3 (3 mm) needles and Brown, cast on 5 sts.

Beg with a k row, work 16 rows in st st.

Bind off.

Loops (Make 2)

With US 2/3 (3 mm) needles and Brown, cast on 3 sts.

K 6 rows.

Bind off.

Right: the tool belt holds a hammer and screwdriver

TOOLS

Screwdriver

With US 2/3 (3 mm) needles and Black, cast on 4 sts.

Beg with a k row, work 6 rows in st st.

Change to Grey.

Next row: K2tog, k2. (3 sts.)

Beg with a p row, work 9 rows in st st.

Break yarn, thread through rem sts and pull up tightly.

Hammer

With US 2/3 (3 mm) needles and Black, cast on 4 sts.

Beg with a k row, work 6 rows in st st.

Change to Grey.

Next row: K2tog, k2. (3 sts.)

Beg with a p row, work 5 rows in st st.

Bind off.

Hammer head

With US 2/3 (3 mm) needles and Grey, cast on 4 sts.

Beg with a k row, work 4 rows in st st.

Next row: K1, k2tog, k1. (3 sts.)

P 1 row.

Bind off.

Sew press stud to ends of belt. Fold pocket strip over and
over again to form small bag with flap and sew row-ends
together. Stitch to belt. Sew loops to belt. Sew seam on
screwdriver. Sew seam on hammer handle and head and
stitch together. Insert screwdriver through one loop of belt
and hammer through the other. Put on doll.

Fairy

Every little girl will delight in this flower fairy fresh from the garden. Her petal skirt and frilly shoes add to her appeal.

plain knitting

★
★
★

SKILL LEVEL:
advanced

MEASUREMENTS
Approximately 11 in. (28 cm) tall

MATERIALS
- 1 x 100 g ball of Sirdar Country Style DK in Lilac 507
- 1 x 100 g ball of Sirdar Country Style DK in Pink 527
- 1 x 100 g ball of Sirdar Country Style DK in Cream 411
- 1 x 50 g ball of Sirdar Snuggly Pearls DK in White 251
- 1 x 25 g ball of Sirdar Toytime DK in Flesh Tone 963
- Oddments of DK yarn in Dark Pink, Green and Brown
- Pair of US 2/3 (3 mm) (use either US 2 or US 3, based on your gauge)

knitting needles
- Stranded embroidery thread in Black, White, Flesh tone and Pink
- Washable toy stuffing
- 3 flower buttons

ABBREVIATIONS
See page 10.

GAUGE
Country Style DK
26 sts and 38 rows to 4 in. (10 cm) measured over stockinette stitch using US 2/3 (3 mm) needles.
Snuggly Pearls DK
24 sts and 42 rows to 4 in. (10 cm) measured over seed stitch using US 2/3 (3 mm) needles.

DOLL

BODY & HEAD
With US 2/3 (3 mm) needles and Pink, cast on 34 sts.
Beg with a k row, work 2 rows in st st.
Next row: K1, [m1, k2] to last st, m1, k1. (51 sts.)
Beg with a p row, work 17 rows in st st.
Place chart
Next row: K20, k across 11 sts of chart on page 110, k20.
Beg with a p row, work the 11 rows of chart in st st.
Shape shoulders
Next row: K13, k2tog, k21, k2tog, k13. (49 sts.)
P 1 row.
Next row: K12, k2tog, k21, k2tog, k12. (47 sts.)

P 1 row.
Next row: K1, [k2tog] to last 2 sts, k2. (25 sts.)
P 1 row.
Change to Flesh Tone and k 1 row.
P 1 row.
Shape head
Next row: K1, [k1, m1] to last st, k1. (48 sts.)
P 1 row.
Next row: K13, m1, k22, m1, k13. (50 sts.)
Beg with a p row, work 21 rows in st st.
Shape top of head
Next row: [K2, k2tog] to last 2 sts, k2. (38 sts.)
P 1 row.
Next row: K1, [k2tog] to last st, k1. (20 sts.)
P 1 row.

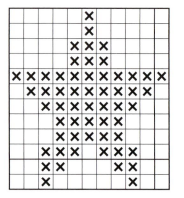

KEY

☒	Lilac
☐	Pink

CHART

Above: *detail of intarsia star*

Next row: [K2tog] to end. (10 sts.)

Next row: [P2tog] to end.

Break yarn (leaving a long length for making up), thread through rem 5 sts and draw up tightly.

LEGS (Make 2)

With US 2/3 (3 mm) needles and Cream, cast on 19 sts.

Beg with a k row, work 24 rows in st st.

Shape instep

Next row: K12, turn.

Next row: P5, turn.

Working on these 5 sts only, work 6 rows in st st.

Change to Dark Pink and work 2 rows in g st.

Break yarn and leave these sts on a spare needle.

With RS facing and Dark Pink, rejoin yarn at base of instep and k up 7 sts down side of instep, k 5 sts from spare needle, k up 7 sts up other side of instep and k rem 7 sts. (33 sts.)

K 3 rows.

Shape sole

Next row: K1, skpo, k10, skpo, k3, k2tog, k10, k2tog, k1. (29 sts.)

K 1 row.

Next row: K1, skpo, k9, skpo, k1, k2tog, k9, k2tog, k1. (25 sts.)

K 1 row.

Next row: K1, skpo, k7, skpo, k2tog, k8, k2tog, k1. (21 sts.)

K 1 row.

Next row: K1, [k2tog] to end. (11 sts.)

K 1 row.

Bind off.

ARMS (Make 2)

With US 2/3 (3 mm) needles and Flesh Tone, cast on 6 sts.

Beg with a k row, work 2 rows in st st.

Next row: K1, m1, k to last st, m1, k1.

P 1 row.

Rep the last 2 rows until there are 18 sts.

Beg with a k row, work 8 rows in st st.

Shape hand

Next row: K9, m1, k9.

P 1 row.

Next row: K9, m1, k1, m1, k9.

P 1 row.

Next row: K9, m1, k3, m1, k9. (23 sts.)

P 1 row.

Next row: K7, [skpo] twice, [k2tog] twice, k8. (19 sts.)

Next row: P7, [p2tog] twice, p8. (17 sts.)

Next row: K7, k2tog, k8. (16 sts.)

P 1 row.

Next row: K1, skpo, k4, k2tog, k4, k2tog, k1. (13 sts.)

P 1 row.

Next row: K1, [k2tog] to end. (7 sts.)

Next row: P1, [p2tog] 3 times. (4 sts.)

Break yarn, thread through rem 4 sts and draw up tightly.

TO MAKE UP

Join center back seam of body and head, leaving the bottom 1¼ in. (4 cm) open for stuffing.

Join sole, heel and center back seam of each leg. Stuff each leg firmly and oversew top edges together. Pin oversewn edges of legs to lower front edge of body. Join lower edge seam of body, catching in the tops of the legs.

Stuff head firmly. Run a draw thread of Pink yarn around neck where color changes, draw up tightly and fasten off. Stuff remainder of body and close seam.

Sew underarm seam of each arm and stuff firmly. Sew to sides of body over shoulder shaping.

CLOTHES

SHOE FRILLS (Make 2)

With US 2/3 (3 mm) needles and Dark Pink, cast on 35 sts.

Beg with a k row, work 2 rows in st st.

Next row: K1, [yon, k2tog] to last 2 sts, k2.

Beg with a p row, work 3 rows in st st.

Bind off.

TO MAKE UP

Fold each frill in half lengthways and sew to upper edges of shoes all the way around the foot. Sew a flower button to the front of each shoe.

SKIRT

Petals (Make 6 Pink, 6 Lilac)

With US 2/3 (3 mm) needles and Pink, cast on 8 sts.

Work in seed st throughout, as follows:

Next row: [K1, p1] to end.

Next row: [P1, k1] to end.

Rep the last 2 rows 7 times more, then the first row once more.

Work 9 rows in seed st, dec 1 st at each end of first and foll two 4th rows. (2 sts.)

Work 1 row.

Next row: K2tog.

Break yarn, thread through rem st and fasten off.

WAISTBAND

With US 2/3 (3 mm) needles and Green, cast on 3 sts.

Next row: K 3, then with RS facing, pick up and k 8 sts along cast-on edge of each Pink petal. (51 sts.)

Next row: Cast on 3 sts, k to end. (54 sts.)

K 3 rows.

Bind off.

TO MAKE UP

Sew a Lilac petal in between each pair of Pink petals on the reverse of the waistband. Stitch ends of the waistband together and sew the last Lilac petal behind the join. Sew the waistband to the doll.

WINGS (Make 2)

With US 2/3 (3 mm) needles and White, cast on 12 sts.

Work in seed st throughout, as follows:

Next row: [K1, p1] to end.

Next row: [P1, k1] to end.

Inc 1 st at each end of every 4th row to 22 sts, incorporating the inc into the patt as set.

Work 4 rows in seed st.

Next row (RS): Patt 2 tog, patt 4, patt 2 tog, turn.

Next row: Patt 2 tog, patt 2, patt 2 tog. (4 sts.)

Bind off in seed st.

With RS facing, rejoin yarn to rem 14 sts and work 4 rows in seed st.

Then, dec 1 st at each end of next and every alt row to 8 sts.

Work 1 row.

Bind off in seed st.

TO MAKE UP

Sew the cast-on edges of the wings together. Place the seam at the center back of the fairy and stitch to the back of the doll.

Hair: Cut 16 in. (40 cm) lengths of Brown yarn and lay on the doll's head. Beginning at the front, sew through all the strands to the right of center to form a side parting. Continue to the crown of the head. Lay more yarn on the back of the head and sew through at the central point.

Smooth down and divide into two bunches. Thread a short length of Dark Pink yarn through each side of the head and tie around each bunch. Knot and secure.

Sew a flower button to hair at front opposite parting.

Embroider eyes in satin stitch using black embroidery thread. Embroider eyelashes using short straight stitches and black embroidery thread. Sew a small white highlight in each eye. Embroider nose in stem stitch using flesh tone embroidery thread. Embroider mouth in stem stitch using pink embroidery thread.

Right: *back view of the fairy showing the sparkly wings*

Princess

A sparkly, pink princess doll; perfect for your own little princess. As her dress is removable why not make a whole wardrobe of sparkly clothes?

plain knitting

⭐
⭐
⭐

SKILL LEVEL:
advanced

MEASUREMENTS
Approximately 11 in. (28 cm) tall

MATERIALS
- 2 x 50 g balls of Twilleys of Stamford Freedom Cotton DK in Pink 04 (A)
- 2 x 50 g balls of Twilleys of Stamford Freedom Cotton DK in White 01 (B)
- 1 x 100 g ball of Twilleys of Stamford Lyscordet in Bright Pink 84 (C)
- 2 x 25 g balls of Twilleys of Stamford Goldfingering in Bright Pink 62 (C)
- 1 x 25 g ball of Twilleys of Stamford Goldfingering in White 01 (D)
- 1 x 25 g ball of Twilleys of Stamford Goldfingering in Gold 04 (E)
- 1 x 25 g ball of Twilleys of Stamford Goldfingering in Gold Mix 14 (F)
- Oddments of Cotton DK yarn in Yellow
- Pair each of US 2 (2¾ mm), US 3 (3¼ mm), and US 6 (4 mm) knitting needles
- US E/4 (3.5 mm) crochet hook

- Stranded embroidery thread in Black, White, Flesh tone and Pink
- Washable toy stuffing
- A hook and eye fastening

ABBREVIATIONS
See page 10.

GAUGE
Freedom Cotton DK
23 sts and 32 rows to 4 in. (10 cm) measured over stockinette stitch using US 3 (3¼ mm) needles
21 sts and 30 rows to 4 in. (10 cm) measured over stockinette stitch using US 6 (4 mm) needles
Goldfingering
30 sts and 40 rows to 4 in. (10 cm) measured over stockinette stitch using US 2 (2¾ mm) needles
Goldfingering & Lyscordet used together
23 sts and 28 rows to 4 in. (10 cm) measured over stockinette stitch using US 6 (4 mm) needles

DOLL

BODY & HEAD
With US 3 (3¼ mm) needles and B, cast on 34 sts.
Beg with a k row, work 2 rows in st st.
Next row: K1, [m1, k2] to last st, m1, k1. (51 sts.)

Beg with a p row, work 7 rows in st st.
Change to A and beg with a k row, work 14 rows in st st.
Shape shoulders
Next row: K13, k2tog, k21, k2tog, k13. (49 sts.)
P 1 row.
Next row: K12, k2tog, k21, k2tog, k12. (47 sts.)
P 1 row.

Next row: K1, [k2tog] to last 2 sts, k2. (25 sts.)

P 1 row.

K 1 row, placing markers at each end of row.

P 1 row.

Shape head

Next row: K1, [k1, m1] to last st, k1. (48 sts.)

P 1 row.

Next row: K13, m1, k22, m1, k13. (50 sts.)

Beg with a p row, work 21 rows in st st.

Shape top of head

Next row: [K2, k2tog] to last 2 sts, k2. (38 sts.)

P 1 row.

Next row: K1, [k2tog] to last st, k1. (20 sts.)

P 1 row.

Next row: [K2tog] to end. (10 sts.)

Next row: [P2tog] to end.

Break yarn (leaving a long length for making up), thread through remaining 5 sts and draw up tightly.

LEGS (Make 2)

With US 3 (3¼ mm) needles and A, cast on 19 sts.

Beg with a k row, work 26 rows in st st.

Shape instep

Next row: K12, turn.

Next row: P5, turn.

Working on these 5 sts only, work 8 rows in st st.

Break yarn and leave these sts on a spare needle.

With RS facing and A, rejoin yarn at base of instep and k up 7 sts down side of instep, k5 sts from spare needle, k up 7 sts up other side of instep and k rem 7 sts. (33 sts.)

Beg with a p row, work 3 rows in st st.

Shape sole

Next row: K1, skpo, k10, skpo, k3, k2tog, k10, k2tog, k1. (29 sts.)

P 1 row.

Next row: K1, skpo, k9, skpo, k1, k2tog, k9, k2tog, k1. (25 sts.)

P 1 row.

Next row: K1, [k2tog] to end. (13 sts.)

P 1 row.

Bind off.

ARMS (Make 2)

With US 3 (3¼ mm) needles and A, cast on 6 sts.

Beg with a k row, work 2 rows in st st.

Next row: K1, m1, k to last st, m1, k1.

P 1 row.

Rep the last 2 rows until there are 18 sts.

Beg with a k row, work 8 rows in st st.

Shape hand

Next row: K9, m1, k9. (19 sts.)

P 1 row.

Next row: K9, m1, k1, m1, k9. (21 sts.)

P 1 row.

Next row: K9, m1, k3, m1, k9. (23 sts.)

P 1 row.

Next row: K7, [skpo] twice, [k2tog] twice, k8. (19 sts.)

Next row: P7, [p2tog] twice, p8. (17 sts.)

Next row: K7, k2tog, k8. (16 sts.)

P 1 row.

Next row: K1, skpo, k4, k2tog, k4, k2tog, k1. (13 sts.)

P 1 row.

Next row: K1, [k2tog] to end. (7 sts.)

Next row: P1, [p2tog] 3 times.

Break yarn, thread through rem 4 sts and draw up tightly.

TO MAKE UP

Join sole, heel and center back seam of each leg. Stuff firmly and oversew top edges together.

Place oversewn edges of legs in bottom edge of body and sew through all thicknesses to catch in legs.

Sew center back seam of head and body, leaving an opening. Stuff head firmly. Run a draw thread of Pink yarn around neck at markers. Draw up tightly and fasten off. Stuff remainder of body and close seam.

Sew underarm seams of each arm. Stuff and sew to sides of body.

Above: *shoes fit for a princess*

CLOTHES

DRESS

Please note: 1 end of Lyscordet and 1 end of Goldfingering used together whenever C is used.

Front

* With US 6 (4 mm) needles and C, cast on 52 sts.

Beg with a k row, work 26 rows in st st.

Shape for bodice

Next row: K1, [k2tog] to last st, k1. (27 sts.) *

Beg with a p row, work 9 rows in st st.

Shape armholes

Bind off 4 sts at beg of next 2 rows. (19 sts.)

Beg with a k row, work 4 rows in st st.

Shape neck

Next row: K6, cast off 7 sts, k6.

Work on these 6 sts only as follows:

Next row: P4, p2tog. (5 sts.)

Next row: K2tog, k3. (4 sts.)

Next row: P2, p2tog. (3 sts.)

Bind off.

With WS facing, rejoin yarn to other side of neck and work as for first side of neck, rev all shapings.

Back

Work as front from * to *.

P 1 row.

Divide for back opening

Next row: K13, turn.

Work on these 13 sts only as follows:

Beg with a p row, work 7 rows in st st.

Shape armhole

Next row: Bind off 4 sts, k to end. (9 sts.)

Beg with a p row, work 6 rows in st st.

Shape neck

Next row: Bind off 4 sts, p to end. (5 sts.)

Next row: K to last 2 sts, k2tog. (4 sts.)

Next row: P2tog, p to end. (3 sts.)

Bind off.

With RS facing, rejoin yarn to rem 14 sts and work as follows:

Beg with a k row, work 9 rows in st st.

Shape armhole

Next row: Bind off 4 sts, p to end. (10 sts.)

Beg with a k row, work 6 rows in st st.

Shape neck

Next row: Bind off 4 sts, k to end. (6 sts.)

Above: *back view of Princess*

Next row: P to last 2 sts, p2tog. (5 sts.)

Next row: K2tog, k to end. (4 sts.)

Bind off.

SLEEVES (Make 2)

With US 2 (2¾ mm) needles and D, cast on 24 sts.

Beg with a k row, work 4 rows in st st.

Picot hem

Next row: K1, [yon, k2tog] to last st, k1.

Beg with a p row, work 3 rows in st st.

Change to US 6 (4 mm) needles and C, beg with a k row, work 4 rows in st st.

Bind off 4 sts at beg of next 2 rows. (16 sts.)

Then dec 1 st at each end of next 2 rows. (12 sts.)

Beg with a k row, work 4 rows in st st.

Bind off.

UNDERSKIRT

With US 6 (4 mm) needles and B, cast on 92 sts.

Beg with a k row, work 34 rows in st st.

Next row: K1, [k2tog] to last st, k1. (47 sts.)

P 1 row.

Bind off.

TO MAKE UP

Join shoulder seams.

Neck edging: With US E/4 (3.5 mm) crochet hook and D, work ss around neck edge and edges of back opening. Fold up picot hem of sleeves and sew to underside. Sew sleeve heads into armholes, gathering to fit. Sew side and sleeve seams of dress. Sew hook and eye to top of back opening.

Hem edging: With US E/4 (3.5 mm) crochet hook and D, work 1 dc into every stitch of cast-on edge of dress. Then 1 dc into 1st dc, [miss 2 dc, 5 tr into next dc, miss 2 dc, 1 dc into next dc] to end. Fasten off.
Join center back seam of underskirt. Work hem edging as for dress.
Sew underskirt to inside of dress at start of bodice.

Sash: With US E/4 (3.5 mm) crochet hook and D, work a 56 cm (22 in.) length of ch.
Next row: 1 dc into every ch to end.
Fasten off.
Tie around waist.

SHOES (Make 2)

With US 2 (2¾ mm) needles and E, cast on 33 sts.
K 2 rows.
Next row: K15, [m1, k1] 3 times, m1, k15. (37 sts.)
Beg with a p row, work 5 rows in st st.
Next row: K1, skpo, k13, skpo, k1, k2tog, k13, k2tog, k1.
P 1 row.
Next row: K1, skpo, k11, skpo, k1, k2tog, k11, k2tog, k1.
P 1 row.
Next row: K1, [k2tog, k1] to last st, k1. (20 sts.)
P 1 row.
Next row: K1, [k2tog] to last st, k1. (11 sts.)
P 1 row.
Bind off.
Join sole and heel seam and place shoes on feet of doll.

HAIR

Cut 18 in. (45 cm) lengths of Yellow yarn and lay on head. Sew to head in a line from front to back of head to form a center parting. Take a small section of hair from each side of head and twist towards the back of the head. Tie a length of yarn around the two sections where they meet at the back and secure. Trim hair to an even length.

TIARA

With US 2 (2¾ mm) needles and F, cast on 22 sts.
Work 2 rows in seed st.
** **Next row:** Patt 6, turn.
Work on these 6 sts only as follows:
Next row: Skpo, patt 2, patt 2 tog.
Work 1 row.
Next row: Skpo, patt 2 tog.
Next row: Work 2 tog.
Break yarn and pull through rem st. **
With RS facing, rejoin yarn to rem sts.
Next row: Patt 10, turn.
Work on these 10 sts only as follows:
Next row: Skpo, patt 6, patt 2 tog.
Patt 1 row.
Next row: Skpo, patt 4, patt 2 tog.
Patt 1 row.
Next row: Skpo, patt 2, patt 2 tog.
Next row: Skpo, patt 2 tog.
Next row: Patt 2 tog.
Break yarn and pull through rem st.
With RS facing, rejoin yarn to rem sts and rep from ** to **.

Sew Tiara to front of doll's head over hair.
Embroider eyes in satin stitch using black embroidery thread. Sew eyelashes in black, using small straight stitches. Sew a small white highlight in each eye. Embroider nose in stem stitch using flesh tone embroidery thread. Embroider mouth in stem stitch using pink embroidery thread.

Above: *detail of face, hair and tiara*

Pirate

Already a firm favorite with my two boys, this swashbuckling pirate is all set to sail the seven seas for some new adventures.

plain knitting

★
★
★

SKILL LEVEL: **advanced**

MEASUREMENTS
Approximately 14½ in. (36 cm) tall

MATERIALS
- 1 x 100 g ball of King Cole Big Value Baby DK in Peach 59
- 1 x 100 g ball of King Cole Woolmix DK in White 1
- 1 x 100 g ball of King Cole Woolmix DK in Red/Ox Blood 307
- 1 x 100 g ball of King Cole Woolmix DK in Royal 21
- 1 x 100 g ball of King Cole Woolmix DK in Black 48
- Oddments of DK yarn in Light Brown
- Pair of US 2/3 (3 mm) (use either US 2 or US 3, based on your gauge) knitting needles
- Stranded embroidery thread in Black, White, Flesh tone and Pink
- Washable toy stuffing
- Scraps of felt in white and yellow

ABBREVIATIONS
See page 10.

GAUGE
Woolmix DK and Big Value Baby DK
25 sts and 34 rows to 4 in. (10 cm) measured over stockinette stitch using US 2/3 (3 mm) needles.

PIRATE

TROUSERS
First leg
* With US 2/3 (3 mm) needles and Royal, cast on 27 sts.
Beg with a k row, work 20 rows in st st. *
Place sts on a spare needle.

Second leg
Work as for first leg from * to *.

Join Legs
K across 27 sts of second leg, then 27 sts of first leg. (54 sts.)
P 1 row.
Next row: K27, m1, k27. (55 sts.)
Beg with a p row, work 9 rows in st st.

Change to Black and work 4 rows in st st.
Change to Red and working stripes of 2 rows Red, 2 rows White throughout, work 16 rows in st st.

Shape shoulders
Cont stripe sequence:
Next row: K13, skpo, k25, k2tog, k13. (53 sts.)
P 1 row.
Next row: K13, skpo, k23, k2tog, k13. (51 sts.)
P 1 row.
Next row: K12, skpo, k23, k2tog, k12. (49 sts.)
P 1 row.
Next row: K1, [k2tog] to last 2 sts, k2. (26 sts.)
P 1 row.
Change to Peach.
Work 2 rows in st st.

Shape head

Next row: K1, [k1, m1] to last st, k1. (50 sts.)

P 1 row.

Next row: K13, m1, k24, m1, k13. (52 sts.)

P 1 row.

Next row: K13, m1, k1, m1, k24, m1, k1, m1, k13. (56 sts.)

Beg with a p row, work 21 rows in st st.

Shape top of head

Next row: K2, [k2, k2tog] to last 2 sts, k2. (43 sts.)

P 1 row.

Next row: K1, [k2tog] to last 2 sts, k2. (23 sts.)

P 1 row.

Next row: K1, [k2tog] to end. (12 sts.)

Next row: [P2tog] to end.

Break yarn (leaving a long length for making up), thread through rem 6 sts and draw up tightly.

TROUSER EDGING

With US 2/3 (3 mm) needles and Royal and with RS facing, k up 27 sts along cast-on edge of one trouser leg.

Next row: Bind off 2 sts, **p5, turn.

Next row: Skpo, k1, k2tog, turn.

Next row: P3, turn.

Next row: Skpo, k1, turn.

Next row: P2tog, break yarn, thread through rem st and pull tightly. **

With WS facing, rejoin yarn to rem sts and rep from ** to **
4 times more.

Rep for other trouser leg.

LEGS (Make 2)

With US 2/3 (3 mm) needles and Peach, cast on 26 sts.

Beg with a k row, work 14 rows in st st.

Shape instep

Next row: K16, turn.

Next row: P6, turn.

Working on these 6 sts only, work 8 rows in st st.

Break yarn and leave these sts on a spare needle.

With RS facing, rejoin yarn at base of instep and k up 7 sts down side of instep, k6 sts from spare needle, k up 7 sts up other side of instep and k rem 10 sts. (40 sts.)

Beg with a p row, work 3 rows in st st.

Shape sole

Next row: K1, skpo, k13, skpo, k4, k2tog, k13, k2tog, k1. (36 sts.)

P 1 row.

Next row: K1, skpo, k12, skpo, k2, k2tog, k12, k2tog, k1. (32 sts.)

P 1 row.

Next row: K1, [k2tog] to last st, k1. (17 sts.)

P 1 row.

Bind off.

ARMS (Make 2)

With US 2/3 (3 mm) needles and Red, cast on 6 sts.

Beg with a k row, work 2 rows in st st.

Working stripes of 2 rows White, 2 rows Red throughout, cont as follows:

Next row: K1, m1, k to last st, m1, k1.

P 1 row.

Rep the last 2 rows until there are 18 sts.

Beg with a k row, work 12 rows in st st.

Change to Peach and beg with a k row, work 6 rows in st st.

Shape hand

Next row: K9, m1, k9. (19 sts.)

P 1 row.

Next row: K9, m1, k1, m1, k9. (21 sts.)

P 1 row.

Next row: K9, m1, k3, m1, k9. (23 sts.)

P 1 row.

Next row: K9, m1, k5, m1, k9. (25 sts.)

P1 row.

Next row: K9, [skpo] twice, [k2tog] twice, k8. (21 sts.)

Next row: P8, [p2tog] twice, p9. (19 sts.)

Left: *the pirate's trousers have a ragged edge*

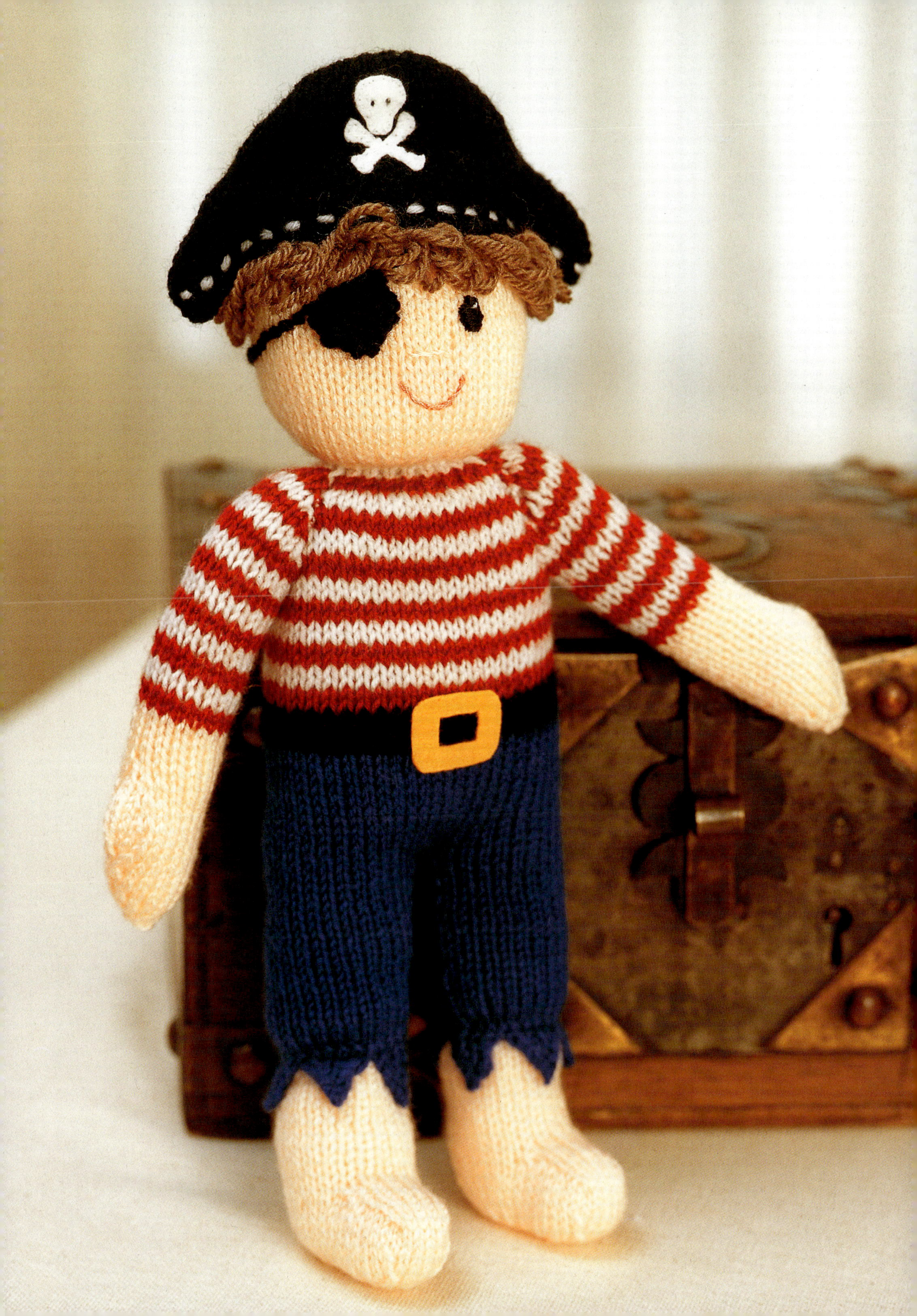

Next row: K9, k2tog, k8. (18 sts.)

P 1 row.

Next row: K1, skpo, k4, [k2tog] twice, k4, k2tog, k1.

P 1 row.

Next row: K1, [k2tog] to last st, k1. (8 sts.)

Next row: [P2tog] 4 times.

Break yarn, thread through rem 4 sts and draw up tightly.

TO MAKE UP

Join inside leg seams and then center back seam of trousers.

Join center back seam of head and body leaving an opening. Stuff head firmly. Run a draw thread of White yarn around neck where color changes, pull tightly and fasten off. Stuff remainder of body and legs. Close opening.

Sew sole, heel and center back seam of each leg. Stuff firmly. Place top edge of each leg inside each trouser leg and join the two together sewing underneath the trouser points. Catch each trouser point down onto legs.

Sew underarm seam of each arm. Stuff and sew to sides of body over shoulder shaping.

Sew loops of Light Brown yarn to head for hair, around hairline at front and back.

Above: detail of face, hair and hat

ACCESSORIES

HAT (Make 2)

With US 2/3 (3 mm) needles and Black, cast on 40 sts.

Beg with a k row, work 6 rows in st st.

Bind off 4 sts at beg of next 4 rows. (24 sts.)

Work 4 rows in st st.

Dec 1 st at each end of next 4 rows. (16 sts.)

Next row: [K2tog] to end. (8 sts.)

Bind off.

TO MAKE UP

Join side and top edges together, following shaping. Using White yarn, sew running stitch all around bottom edge of hat. Sew lower edges of hat together at each side for 1 in. (2.5 cm). Cut skull and cross bones from white felt using the pattern below (actual size) and sew to front of hat.

PATCH

With US 2/3 (3 mm) needles and Black, cast on 6 sts.

K 3 rows.

Next row: Skpo, k2, k2tog. (4 sts.)

K 1 row.

Next row: Skpo, k2tog. (2 sts.)

Bind off.

TO MAKE UP

Sew patch to face where the right eye should be. Starting at each upper corner of the patch, work stem stitch in Black yarn around side of face and up into hair.

Place hat on doll's head and sew all around at hairline.

Cut belt buckle from yellow felt using the pattern below (actual size) and sew to front of doll over black belt.

Embroider eye in satin stitch using black embroidery thread. Sew a small white highlight in eye. Work nose and mouth in stem stitch, using flesh tone and pink respectively.

SKULL AND CROSS BONE

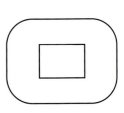

BUCKLE

Cowboy

Straight from the Wild West and into the heart of your little cowboy! Hours of fun are guaranteed with this little chap.

MEASUREMENTS
Approximately 14 in. (35 cm) tall

MATERIALS
- 1 x 100 g ball of King Cole Big Value Baby DK in Peach 59
- 1 x 100 g ball of King Cole Woolmix DK in White 1
- 1 x 100 g ball of King Cole Woolmix DK in Red/Ox Blood 307
- 1 x 100 g ball of King Cole Big Value Baby DK in Jeans 207
- Small amounts of King Cole Big Value DK in Taupe 37 and Russett 60
- Oddments of DK yarn in yellow
- Pair of US 2/3 (3 mm) (use either US 2 or US 3, based on your gauge) knitting needles
- Stranded embroidery thread in Black, Orange, White, Flesh tone and Pink
- Washable toy stuffing

ABBREVIATIONS
See page 10.

GAUGE
25 sts and 34 rows to 4 in. (10 cm) measured over stockinette stitch using US 2/3 (3 mm) needles.

COWBOY

TROUSERS
First leg
* With US 2/3 (3 mm) needles and Jeans, cast on 27 sts.
K 2 rows.
Beg with a k row, work 22 rows in st st. *
Place sts on a spare needle.
Second leg
Work as for first leg from * to *.
Join Legs
K across 27 sts of second leg, then 27 sts of first leg. (54 sts.)
P 1 row.
Next row: K27, m1, k27. (55 sts.)
Beg with a p row, work 9 rows in st st.

Change to Russett and work 4 rows in st st.
Change to White and patt as follows:
** **Row 1:** K3 White, [k1 Red, k2 White] to last 4 sts, k1 Red, k3 White.
Row 2: P3 White, [p1 Red, p2 White] to last 4 sts, p1 Red, p3 White.
Row 3: K all sts Red.
Row 4: As Row 2.
Row 5: As Row 1.
Row 6: P all sts Red. **
These 6 rows form patt, rep from ** to ** once more.
Then, work Rows 1 to 4 of patt again.

Shape shoulders
Cont patt as set, incorporating dec into patt.
Next row: K13, skpo, k25, k2tog, k13. (53 sts.)
P 1 row.
Next row: K13, skpo, k23, k2tog, k13. (51 sts.)

Above: *detail of legs and boots*

P 1 row.
Next row: K12, skpo, k23, k2tog, k12. (49 sts.)
P 1 row.
Next row: K1, [k2tog] to last 2 sts, k2. (26 sts.)
P 1 row.
Change to Peach.
Work 2 rows in st st.

Shape head
Next row: K1, [k1, m1] to last st, k1. (50 sts.)
P 1 row.
Next row: K13, m1, k24, m1, k13. (52 sts.)
P 1 row.
Next row: K13, m1, k1, m1, k24, m1, k1, m1, k13. (56 sts.)
Beg with a p row, work 21 rows in st st.

Shape top of head
Next row: K2, [k2, k2tog] to last 2 sts, k2. (43 sts.)
P 1 row.
Next row: K1, [k2tog] to last 2 sts, k2. (23 sts.)
P 1 row.

Next row: K1, [k2tog] to end. (12 sts.)
Next row: [P2tog] to end.
Break yarn (leaving a long length for making up), thread through rem 6 sts and draw up tightly.

BOOTS (Make 2)
With US 2/3 (3 mm) needles and Russett, cast on 26 sts.
Beg with a k row, work 10 rows in st st.
Shape instep
Next row: K16, turn.
Next row: P6, turn.
Working on these 6 sts only, work 8 rows in st st.
Break yarn and leave these sts on a spare needle.
With RS facing, rejoin yarn at base of instep and k up 7 sts down side of instep, k 6 sts from spare needle, k up 7 sts up other side of instep and k rem 10 sts. (40 sts.)
Beg with a p row, work 3 rows in st st.
Shape sole
Next row: K1, skpo, k13, skpo, k4, k2tog, k13, k2tog, k1. (36 sts.)
P 1 row.
Next row: K1, skpo, k12, skpo, k2, k2tog, k12, k2tog, k1. (32 sts.)
P 1 row.
Next row: K1, [k2tog] to last st, k1. (17 sts.)
P 1 row.
Bind off.

ARMS (Make 2)
With US 2/3 (3 mm) needles and White, cast on 6 sts.
Row 1: [K2 White, k1 Red] twice.
Row 2: [P1 Red, p2 White] twice.
Row 3: All sts Red, k1, m1, k to last st, m1, k1. (8 sts.)
Row 4: P1 White, [p1 Red, p2 White] to last st, p1 Red.
Row 5: K1, m1 Red, [k2 White, k1 Red] to last st, m1, k1 White. (10 sts.)
Row 6: P all sts Red.
Row 7: K1, m1 White, [k1 Red, k2 White] to last 3 sts, k1 Red, k1, m1, k1 White. (12 sts.)
Row 8: [P1 Red, p2 White] to end.
Row 9: As Row 3. (14 sts.)
Row 10: P1 White, [p1 Red, p2 White] to last st, p1 Red.
Row 11: As Row 5.
Row 12: As Row 6.

Right: *back view showing the stitching on the Cowboy's jeans*

Row 13: K1, m1 White, [k1 Red, k2 White] to last 3 sts, k1 Red, k1, m1, k1 White. (18 sts.)
Row 14: P3 White, [p1 Red, p2 White] to end.
Beg with a k row, and patt as set, work 16 rows in st st without shaping.
Change to Peach.
Shape hand
Next row: K9, m1, k9. (19 sts.)
P 1 row.
Next row: K9, m1, k1, m1, k9. (21 sts.)
P 1 row.
Next row: K9, m1, k3, m1, k9. (23 sts.)
P 1 row.
Next row: K9, m1, k5, m1, k9. (25 sts.)
P 1 row.
Next row: K9, [skpo] twice, [k2tog] twice, k8. (21 sts.)
Next row: P8, [p2tog] twice, p9. (19 sts.)
Next row: K9, k2tog, k8. (18 sts.)
P 1 row.
Next row: K1, skpo, k4, [k2tog] twice, k4, k2tog, k1.
P 1 row.
Next row: K1, [k2tog] to last st, k1. (8 sts.)
Next row: [P2tog] 4 times.
Break yarn, thread through rem 4 sts and draw up tightly.

TO MAKE UP
Join inside leg and center back seam of trousers.
Join center back seam of body and head, leaving an opening. Stuff head firmly. Run a draw thread of Red yarn around neck where color changes, pull tightly and fasten off. Stuff remainder of body and legs and close opening.
Sew sole, heel and center back seam of each boot. Stuff firmly and place inside trouser legs. Stitch together all around bottom of trousers.
Sew arm seams. Stuff firmly and stitch to sides of body.
Swiss darn belt loops in Denim yarn at right and left front and back. Swiss darn belt buckle in Yellow yarn. Using orange embroidery thread and running stitch, sew lines down sides of each leg, curves for front pockets and fly, and western pockets on back.

CLOTHES

WAISTCOAT
Back
With US 2/3 (3 mm) needles and Taupe, cast on 29 sts.
K 2 rows.
Beg with a k row, work 4 rows in st st.
Shape armholes
Dec 1 st at each end of the next and every foll k row to 15 sts.
P 1 row, k 1 row.
Bind off.

Left front
With US 2/3 (3 mm) needles and Taupe, cast on 4 sts.
K 1 row.
Next row: K2, [m1] twice, k2. (6 sts.)
Next row (RS): K2, m1, k to last 2 sts, m1, k2.

Next row: K2, m1, p to last 2 sts, m1, k2.

Rep the last 2 rows once more. (14 sts.)

K 1 row.

Next row: K2, p to end.

Rep the last 2 rows once more.

Shape armhole

Next row: K2, skpo, k to last 4 sts, k2tog, k2.

Next row: K2, p to last 2 sts, k2.

Rep the last 2 rows until 2 sts rem. (When only 6 sts rem, k every row.)

Bind off.

Right front

Make as for left front, except work g st edge at right edge.

TO MAKE UP

Join side and shoulder seams and place on doll.

HAT
Side

With US 2/3 (3 mm) needles and Russett, cast on 58 sts.

Beg with a k row, work 12 rows in st st.

Next row: K3, [k2tog, k8] to last 5 sts, k2tog, k3. (52 sts.)

Beg with a p row, work 3 rows in st st.

Bind off.

Top

With US 2/3 (3 mm) needles and Russett, cast on 5 sts.

Beg with a k row, work 15 rows in st st, inc 1 st at each end of every 3rd row. (15 sts.)

Beg with a p row, work 3 rows in st st.

Then, beg with a k row, work 4 rows in st st, dec 1 st at each end of 2nd and 4th rows. (11 sts.)

Now, cast off 2 sts at beg of next 2 rows. (7 sts.)

Bind off.

Brim

With US 2/3 (3 mm) needles and Russett, cast on 10 sts.

Row 1: K8, turn.

Row 2: K to end.

Row 3: K9, turn.

Row 4: K to end.

Row 5: K all sts.

Row 6: K all sts.

Rep the last 6 rows 25 times more.

Bind off.

TO MAKE UP

Join row-ends of side together. Then sew to hat top, placing seam of side section in center of cast-off edge of hat top.

Sew short ends of brim together. Sew brim to bottom edge of hat side.

Hair: Cut 2½ in. (6 cm) lengths of Yellow yarn. Lay vertically all around head, placing the top end just above the hairline, and sew to head.

Place hat over hair and sew hat to head, covering the top ends of hair.

Loosely tack sides of hat brim to side of hat.

Embroider eyes in satin stitch using black embroidery thread. Sew a small white highlight in each eye. Embroider nose in stem stitch using flesh tone embroidery thread. Embroider mouth in stem stitch using pink embroidery thread.

Left: *detail showing shirt, waistcoat, head and hat*

useful addresses

YARN SUPPLIERS

As hand knitting yarns are largely fashion led, yarns and colors which are in a shade card one year may not be in there the following year. Therefore, please check yarn availability and stockists with the following suppliers.

Alpaca Select
82 Frobisher Road
Coventry
CV3 6NA
Tel: +44 (0)24 7641 1776
Fax: +44 (0)24 7669 2496
www.alpacaselect.co.uk
Email: sales@alpacaselect.co.uk
Worldwide mail order available direct

Jaeger Handknits
Green Lane Mill
Holmfirth
West Yorkshire
HD9 2DX
Tel: +44 (0)1484 680050
Contact for stockists

Jamieson & Smith (Shetland Wool Brokers) Ltd
90 North Road
Lerwick
Shetland Isles
ZE1 0PQ
Tel: +44 (0)1595 693579
Fax: +44 (0) 1595 695009
www.shetland-wool-brokers.zetnet.co.uk
Email:
Shetland.wool.brokers@zetnet.co.uk
Worldwide mail order available direct

King Cole Ltd
Merrie Mills
Elliott Street
Silsden, nr Keighley
West Yorkshire
BD20 0DE
Tel: +44 (0)1535 650230
Fax: +44 (0) 1535 650240
www.kingcole.co.uk
Email UK sales & enquiries:
lance.martin@kingcole.co.uk
Email export sales & enquiries:
tom.holmes@kingcole.co.uk

Wendy & Peter Pan
Thomas B. Ramsden & Co. Ltd
Netherfield Road
Guiseley
West Yorkshire
LS20 9PD
Tel: +44 (0)1943 872264
Fax: +44 (0)1943 878689
www.tbramsden.co.uk
Email: sales@tbramsden.co.uk

Rowan
Green Lane Mill
Holmfirth
West Yorkshire
HD9 2DX
Tel: +44 (0)1484 681881
Fax: +44 (0) 1484 687920
www.knitrowan.com
Email: mail@knitrowan.com
Contact for stockists or order online

Sirdar
Sirdar Spining Ltd
Flanshaw Lane
Alverthorpe
Wakefield
West Yorkshire
WF2 9ND
Tel: +44 (0)1924 371501
Fax: +44 (0)1924 290506
www.sirdar.co.uk
Email: consumer@sirdar.co.uk

Twilleys of Stamford
Roman Mill
Little Casterton Road
Stamford
Lincs
PE9 1BG
Tel: +44 (0)1780 752661
Fax: +44 (0)1780 765215
www.tbramsden.co.uk
Email: twilleys@tbramsden.co.uk

UK Alpaca Ltd
Vulscombe Farm
Cruwys Morchard
Tiverton
Devon
EX16 8NB
Telephone: +44 (0)1884 243579
Fax: +44 (0) 1884 243514
www.ukalpaca.com
Email: sales@ukalpaca.com
Worldwide mail order available direct

OTHER MATERIALS

The DMC Company
77 South Hackensack Ave
Bldg 10F
South Kearny
NJ 07032
Tel: 973-589-0606
www.dmc-usa.com
Embroidery thread available from stockists worldwide. Contact for stockists details

Needles, crochet hooks, stuffing, ribbons, buttons etc available from needlework shops and knitting/crochet areas in department stores, worldwide.

index

acknowledgements

My grateful thanks go to the following:

Laura Bolton and Lance Martin at King Cole, Pauline Brown at Sirdar, Ann Hinchcliffe at Rowan and Jaeger, Rosemarie Fordham at Twilleys of Stamford, T. B. Ramsdens, Juliet Sensicle at UK Alpaca, Isabel Langdon at Alpaca Select, and Oliver Henry and Donna at Jamieson & Smith.

The brilliant knitters: Margaret Dayman, Kate Foster, Alys Ackerman, Joyce Jackson and Nina Jackson.

Shona Wood for her beautiful photographs, Lisa Tai for designing the book, and Sue Horan for checking all the patterns.

Cara Ackerman at DMC. Rosemary Wilkinson for giving me this opportunity and your guidance. Clare Sayer for all your hard work, help and patience.

My two sons; Elliot and Leo for being my toy testers, and my husband Mark for your unerring love, help and support.